Mind-Controlled Sex Slaves And the CIA

A Collection of Essays and Interviews About Project MONARCH

by
Tracy R. Twyman

Mind-Controlled Sex Slaves
By Tracy R. Twyman
ISBN 978-1-962312-05-9

Copyright 2008
Dragon Key Press
USA
All right reserved.

For more information, visit:

dragonkeypress.com
tracyrtwyman.com

Acknowledgements

Special thanks to all of those who made this book possible, including Brian Albert, John DeCamp, Pamela Freyd, Noreen Gosch, Ted Gunderson, Cathy O'Brien, and Mark Philips.

Contents

The Stepford Whores: Project MONARCH and Mind-Controlled Sex Slaves

By Tracy R. Twyman

In the months preceding September 11th 2001, the airwaves of cable news channels were filled with the saga of Congressman Gary Condit, and the cover-up of his affair with intern Chandra Levy. Levy disappeared on April 30, 2001-- Walpurgisnacht--the most sacred witch holiday on the calendar. Condit's not-very-forthcoming statements on the matter, coupled with the fact that Chandra appeared to be on her way to visit him on the night she disappeared led to speculation that he was somehow involved with her kidnapping and/or death. This speculation reached a fevered pitch when bizarre details of Condit's sex life began to mount. Twenty-seven other women came forth claiming to have had sexual relations with the Congressman, including two women (15-years-old at the time), who claimed that he had violently raped them while still a State Assemblyman. Condit was described by one attorney involved in the case as "a serial predator of women." One of the women, Torrie Hendley, who met the leather-clad Condit at a Harley Davidson convention, revealed in an interview with *The Globe* tabloid newspaper that Condit enjoyed kinky, sadomasochistic sex, referring to his many ladies as his "sex slaves." She also said that he insisted on using code names with these women while talking on the phone, and refused to wear condoms, stating to Ms. Hendley that "there's a cure for AIDS, anyway."

Following the media blitz of the Clinton-Lewinski sex scandal, and then the Condit-Levy affair, many people began to wonder: Why do so many men in positions of power require lots of sex with a variety of people? And where do such men get this sense of entitlement, this attitude that they should be continually provided with a harem of sexual servants, maintained, oftentimes, at taxpayers' expense? Few, if any journalists brought up the amazing similarity between the story of Gary Condit's "sex slaves" and the stories of dozens of men and women who claim to have been forced into sexual slavery for the wealthy and powerful by none other than our own Central Intelligence Agency, through an offshoot of the MK-ULTRA mind control program known as Project MONARCH.

It is well-known now in most literate circles, from declassified documents available through the Freedom of Information Act, that the CIA engaged in a number of covert experiments in mind control, often on unwitting subjects, throughout the 50s, 60s, and 70s as part of a program known as MK-ULTRA. Thus, for example, we have the familiar stories of soldiers in Vietnam being subjected to involuntary testing of the effects of L.S.D. and other drugs on battlefield performance. MK-ULTRA had its roots in Project PAPERCLIP, a post-WWII operation authorized by Harry Truman, in which top scientists from Nazi Germany were smuggled into the United States to work with NASA, the military, and the intelligence community. Their newly acquired knowledge of mind control techniques had come from their experiments on prisoners in Nazi concentration camps, in which, according to experts, they learned of the effects of the calculated use of torture, drugs, hypnotism, electroshock, and sleep deprivation on an individual personality.

According to some, the result was found to be a fragmenting of the personality into separate components which are unaware of one another, creating what is known today as "Multiple Personality Disorder," or by the more recent, clinically-accepted term, "Dissociative Identity Disorder." The individual personality components could then be programmed to perform certain tasks, much like a computer. According to former FBI agent and mind control expert Ted Gunderson: "It's a combination of torture, hypnosis, drugs. And what happens is, they torture them so much, that their personality splits in order to endure the pain and misery. When their personality splits, they [become] another person, and it's through this technique that they train them." Such techniques could, says Gunderson, create Manchurian candidates, unwitting agents of espionage who could courier sensitive messages and even commit assassinations against their will, without any recollection of these events.

For instance, consider the case of Candy Jones, a popular New York pin-up model who one day suddenly recovered repressed memories of having been used as a hypnotic courier for the government (i.e., mind control.) As most forms of hypnosis usually do, mind control training involves the use of "Neuro-Linguistic Programming," teaching the brain to associate certain words or sounds with the performance of certain actions, both mental and physical. Under this definition, teaching your dog to "roll over" on command is Neuro-Linguistic Programming, although a more covert method would involve training him to roll over every time you said "ice cream," and then to forget about the whole event as soon as you snap your fingers.

Although clearly unethical, such practices were justified by the CIA under the belief that the Soviets, America's new arch-enemy, already possessed such covert weaponry of the mind. Former Nebraska State Senator John DeCamp, author of the book *The Franklin Cover-Up*, recalls a conversation with Former CIA Director William Colby regarding the subject. "What he … [said] … was [that] after the Korean War, the American CIA and the American government, in fact, were very terrified. We believed that the ability of other countries, particularly China, Russia, North Korea … their ability in "brainwashing," as it was known at the time, and mind control was developed to such a degree … you can imagine how dangerous that was, and we decided we couldn't afford to be behind. For the very salvation of the country we had to catch up. And so millions and billions were poured into these programs … He said, 'I'll tell you one thing, John. When all is said and done, we were never behind, and we aren't today.'"

Indeed, according to many self-proclaimed victims of mind control, we are well ahead of the game today, and most say the CIA's motivation was never strictly "for the good of the country." For instance, consider the rumored existence of "Project MONARCH," the alleged offshoot of MK-ULTRA designed to create legions of so-called "mind-controlled sex slaves" for use by the rich and powerful. According to conspiracy theorist Fritz Springmeier, the project was called MONARCH after the butterfly of the same name. Training begins in early childhood, when, he says "Children who are traumatized have their legs tied and are electro-shocked and tortured until the alters (personalities) believe they are butterflies." The whole program is based on the "Marionette Programming" purportedly perfected in Nazi Germany with the same aim as MONARCH, in which sex slaves were created who believed themselves to be puppets ("marionettes") controlled by cruel masters.

The value of a mind-controlled sex slave is multi-faceted. For one thing, they can be used to satisfy the perversions of people in positions of power without jeopardizing that power, since a person under mind control is not likely to expose the event to public scrutiny. Furthermore, these encounters can be videotaped for the purpose of blackmailing public officials and businessmen should they at any time step out of line, or do anything to endanger the intelligence community's global plan. (Some people who purport the existence of Project MONARCH might also believe that the CIA is under the control of the Illuminati "New World Order" conspiracy of global domination.)

Then there is the financial aspect. A sex slave can be prostituted from childhood on to wealthy individuals who will pay large sums of money for the experience. They can also be used in child pornography to be sold on the global market. Many MONARCH "survivors" claim that unwanted, expendable sex slaves are picked to star in the most controversial pictures of all-- snuff films, the existence of which has yet to be proven according to the FBI. The slaves are also, say the stories, used as drug mules for the CIA's secret trafficking of illegal substances.

The money derived from these black market transactions of drugs and sex is used, they say, to fund the CIA's many top secret and under-budgeted black operations, as well as to line the pockets of the perpetrators. Potential slaves are chosen for their genetic propensity for suggestibility, hypnotizability, dissociation, and high intelligence. In the past ten years or more, a number of these so-called "survivors" have "recovered" their memories and come forward about their past abuse at the hands of the government. Many have written books, such as Brice Taylor's *Thanks for the Memories: The Truth Has Set Me Free*, Annie McKenna's *Paperclip Dolls*, and Cathy O'Brien's *The TRANCE Formation of*

America. Of these, Cathy O'Brien is perhaps the most well-known.

It's hard to think of a catchier opening line for a chapter than one that includes the words, "substituting his penis for my mother's nipple." Cathy couldn't think of a better one either as she described how her "pedophile" father, Earl O'Brien, allegedly first began to train her sexually. Cathy claims to have come from a family of multi-generational incest perpetrators, where daddy abused all of the kids, and all of the kids abused each other. Growing up in Muskegon, Michigan, a "pedophile capital," according to Cathy, it wasn't long before Cathy's father was whoring her around for use in lucrative child pornography. In time, Mr. O'Brien was caught, but instead of going to jail, he was visited, says Cathy, by future President Gerald Ford, who offered him a deal: sell Cathy into the MONARCH program, and receive immunity from prosecution. The CIA allegedly had good reason to seek Cathy out because, she says, "…they knew that any child that was sexually abused to that extent would be suffering from this dissociative disorder that they were interested in targeting for mind control."

And so her formal MONARCH training began. "Not long after that," she explains in her book, "my father was flown to Boston for a two-week course at Harvard on how to raise me for …Project MONARCH." From then on, Cathy was prostituted to a long list of high-ranking individuals, such as Michigan State Senator Guy Vander Jagt, Canadian Prime Minister Pierre Trudeau, West Virginia Senator Robert Byrd (who later became her "owner" or "controller"), and the aforementioned Gerald Ford. She claims she was forced to engage in all sorts of strange perversions, from having sex with dogs to waving a small American flag with her rectum. This, coupled with her father's constant abuse and torture, kept her in a constant state of dissociation.

According to Cathy, she was controlled with form of Neuro-Linguistic Programming used on many MONARCH slaves, which involved the use of themes from *Wizard of Oz*, and various Disney children's films. She was taught to go into another dimension "over the rainbow" whenever the pain of the abuse became too much to bear, and to identify with Cinderella when her father assigned her a strict daily regimen of household chores, which was part of her slave programming. The hallucinogenic and multi-dimensional themes of *Alice in Wonderland* were also quite extensively used. This was done, not just to Cathy, but to all her brothers and sisters as well, who were also being used in the program. As she writes in her book, "My brother, now 37, remains psychologically locked into those traumatic childhood years and is obsessed with Disney themes and productions to this day. His house is decorated in Disney memorabilia, he wears Disney clothes, listens to my father's instructions on a Disney telephone, and maintains "When You Wish Upon a Star" as his favorite song, which has locked his children into the same theme."

Interestingly, the Disney programming claim is one made by almost every "recovered" MONARCH slave, although it's difficult to determine whether these claims began to surface before or after the publication of Cathy's book. For example, a number of them say that they were taken to Tinker Air Force Base in Oklahoma, where they were placed in electrified "Tinkerbell" cages, and tortured into creating child alters that would, like Peter Pan, never grow up.

However, Cathy did grow up, and although supposedly subjected to daily sexual abuse and torture, she managed to maintain an "A" average throughout her scholastic career, "because when trauma occurs that's too horrible to comprehend," says Cathy, "the brain automatically goes into its own mode, and photographically records events surrounding the trauma … Since I was being traumatized all the time, I was photographically recording what I was being taught in school. So I got excellent grades." Throughout her childhood, she was isolated from society and popular culture, with the exception of the Disney movies previously mentioned, and was heavily exposed to country music. According to Cathy, the country music scene is heavily infiltrated by MONARCH operatives, because the tours they travel in throughout North America easily facilitate the trade of slaves and drugs.

When Cathy got older, she was married off by "The

Company" to Wayne Cox, who fathered her daughter, Kelly (also a mind-controlled sex slave.) Later, she was married a second time to country music MC Alex Houston. Concurrently, she was also symbolically married to Senator Robert Byrd, who became her "controller," and largely dictated the events of her life from then on. She was sent to a sex slave training camp called "Charm School," directed, she says, by Pennsylvania Governor Dick Thornburgh and Ohio State Representative James Traficant [now in prison for bribery and racketeering]. After she graduated, Cathy says, she became a so-called "Presidential Model," and was used to satisfy the sadistic sexual needs of executive-level members of government. From that point forward, the "Who's Who" list of johns she allegedly serviced became exponentially more impressive. She says she was nearly choked to death a number of times by Dick Cheney's enormous penis, and was violently raped by both Cheney and George Bush Sr., after being chased through the woods in a form of human hunting called "The Most Dangerous Game." She claims to have serviced both Bill and Hillary Clinton while the former was still Governor of Arkansas. She says she drove Hillary into a fit of ecstasy with the "Witch's Face" that her handlers had carved into her vagina which, says Cathy, "can give men pleasure," much like ribbed condoms do for women.

Cathy even claims that *Hustler*'s Larry Flynt was part of the conspiracy, and that he hired a photographer named Jimmy Walker to take pornographic pictures of her wedding night with Alex Houston, then had the photos published in one of his magazines. Writes Cathy, "Flynt was unequivocally the official White House Pornographer. [He] maintained … New World Order colleagues such as Presidents Reagan, Bush, and Ford, CIA Director Bill Casey, U.N. Ambassador Madeleine Albright, Senators Byrd and Spector, Congressmen Traficant and VanderJagt, Governors Thornburgh, Blanchard, and Alexander, and various world leaders such as Prime Minister of Canada Mulroney, President of Mexico de la Madrid, and Saudi Arabian King Fahd … to name a few." All of these people, by the way, are on Cathy's list of sexual assailants as well.

And another thing. Cathy O'Brien (like Brice Taylor, and a

number of other proclaimed "Presidential Models") says that none of these high-ranking rapists ever used a condom, because both they and the Presidential Models had been inoculated against all sexually transmitted diseases. Says Cathy, "there was quite a bit of confidence surrounding the fact, and it was a known fact, that since I was used on a White House/Pentagon level … they would not get AIDS from me, because I was 'clean.' That was the term used."

And what was it that Gary Condit reportedly said to Torrie Hendley? "There's a cure for AIDS, anyway."

One of the consistencies that runs through almost all of the personal testimonies of the self-proclaimed MONARCH victims is the use of the occult and Satanism as a "trauma base." Cathy O'Brien vividly describes the "Rite to Remain Silent" she claims she endured at St. Francis of Assisi Church in Muskegon, a reversal of the Catholic mass in which she was allegedly doused in the blood of a freshly-slaughtered lamb and made to take an oath of secrecy. She also claims to have witnessed human sacrifices at Bohemian Grove retreat, an exclusive retreat for global movers and shakers, who meet on a private island every year in secret. They dress up in bizarre costumes and indulge in their most extreme perversions with mind-controlled "Stepford Whores," much like scenes from the Stanley Kubrick film *Eyes Wide Shut*.

Brice Taylor, who claims to have bedded down every President except since John Kennedy (except Carter and Nixon), also says that she experienced similar rituals throughout her abuse, including those involving human sacrifices, anti-Christian night services at Christian churches, being buried alive in a coffin, and being hung upon a cross. Annie McKenna has recovered numerous memories, she says, of her MONARCH-trained family donning dark hoods, chanting, and performing strange rites in graveyards. Even her own children, the first of which she had at age 11, were sacrificed to the blood cult. Writes McKenna, "The ritual abuse served two purposes. First, it exposed a child to horrific trauma, which caused the child to dissociate and create alters. Secondly, the belief was that if we ever did remember, the ritual abuse memories would surface first, and the medical community and public would label us insane."

The claims of mind control and MONARCH programming are just the latest details to be grafted onto the tales of Satanic Ritual Abuse (or SRA) that began to surface in the early 1980s. Although now largely discredited by the mental health establishment, SRA has long been a pervasive urban myth, if nothing more. Many groups, several of them affiliated with Protestant churches, believe in a large conspiracy of Satanists that spans the globe, and which controls the drug and child pornography industry (i.e., the Mafia), as well as, to the view of many, the government (i.e., the "Illuminati"). They believe that these people engage in the large-scale abduction and abuse of thousands of children for use in their sick, sadistic, Satanic sex rituals, and the pornographic documentation thereof. When not from "multi-generational Satanic families," like Taylor's and O'Brien's, where their parents willingly submit them to the MONARCH program, children are supposedly snatched off the streets--the familiar milk carton kids. According to the lore, the conspirators even infiltrate pre-schools and day care centers to access children there.

Ted Gunderson has personally investigated the famous McMartin Pre-School SRA case, even going so far as to hire an archeologist to dig for underground tunnels reported by the children. The children reported that in these tunnels they were subjected to sexual abuse, animal sacrifices, and Disney-based mind control programming by, among others, Steve Garvey, Chuck Norris, and Raymond Buckey, the school's owner. Gunderson claims, "we found the tunnels under the school. … We found 2000 animal bones …" Gunderson believes wholeheartedly that, "The Satanic cult movement dovetails with U.S. intelligence … in addition to being involved in … kidnapping, they were taking kids out of Boy's Town, and out of foster homes and orphanages, and flying them … to Washington, D.C. for sex orgy parties with congressmen and senators. Barney Frank … [has] been identified by the kids, and George Bush Sr. has been at the parties while he was Vice-President. …[We're] talking about a large-scale pedophile ring, and a large-scale kidnapping ring … known as "The Finders." It's a CIA covert operation running out of Washington, D.C. … that's just a cover name for finding children..."

"The Finders" and Project MONARCH were implicated in Nebraska's "Franklin Cover-Up," also investigated by Gunderson, and by the author of *The Franklin Cover-Up*, former State Senator John DeCamp. In a civil case against 16 people, including Laurence E. King (manager of the failed Franklin Savings and Loan), Harold Anderson (publisher of the *Omaha World Herald*), and the Omaha Police Department, plaintiff Paul Bonacci was awarded $1 million by U.S. District Court Judge Warren Urbom in February 1999. In reference to King, the Judge found that he had "continually subjected the plaintiff to repeated sexual assault, false imprisonment, infliction of extreme emotional distress, organized and directed Satanic rituals, forced the plaintiff to 'scavenge' for children to be part of the defendant King's sexual abuse and pornography ring, forced the plaintiff to engage in numerous sexual contacts with the defendant King and others, and participate in deviant sexual games and masochistic orgies with minor children."

Bonacci testified that he was flown on hundreds of trips to Washington, D.C., Kansas City, Chicago, Minnesota, and Los Angeles, where he was taken to "thousands" of pedophilic and sadomasochistic parties, drugged, and prostituted to the rich and powerful. Bonacci admits to participating in the kidnapping of then-12-year-old paper boy Johnny Gosch in Des Moines, Iowa, a story profiled extensively on *America's Most Wanted* and a number of other television programs. Johnny's mother, Noreen Gosch is convinced that Bonacci is telling the truth, and is also convinced that her son was kidnapped by joint intelligence-organized crime elements involved in Project MONARCH. Says Noreen, "[Bonacci] told us that he was put into MONARCH training at a very young age, right at Offutt Air Force Base … Johnny … was put through the same training …" In 1999, Johnny Gosch, a grown man at that point, came to visit his mother for a brief, covert visit in the middle of the night. "He told me that he had been subjected to mind control … and that his job was to compromise politicians, and any VIP that they felt they wanted to do that to … He only mentioned the Satanic rituals briefly."

One of the accused perpetrators who has been implicated by Noreen Gosch, Paul Bonacci, Cathy O'Brien, and a host of other "MONARCH victims" is Lt. Col. Michael Aquino, a former Green Beret and senior U.S. military intelligence officer once involved in the study of "PSY-OPS," or psychological warfare. He wrote an extensive essay with Colonel Paul E. Vallely (a Fox News Channel analyst) called "From PSY-OP to MindWar: The Psychology of Victory." In this essay, the authors advocated the use of propaganda, subliminal messages, air ionization, and ELF waves (i.e., putting low frequency signals in TV and radio broadcasts to induce specific states of mind) in times of war, both domestically and abroad, in order to manipulate public opinion of the war. Another interesting fact about Michael Aquino: He just happens to be the leader and founder of the Temple of Set, a splinter group of the Church of Satan, in which Aquino was once a high-ranking member. The Temple of Set now has a number of chapters that operate on military bases. Interestingly, this group's rituals often involve Nazi symbols and rhetoric, and Aquino once performed a Satanic "working" at Heinrich Himmler's castle of Wewelsburg while in Germany on "official NATO business."

Predictably, this has caused no shortage of controversy to surround Michael Aquino. In the late 1980s, a Satanic Ritual Abuse/Child Sexual Abuse scandal broke out at a day care center on the Presidio military base in San Francisco, where Aquino was stationed. The children identified Aquino, as well as a Baptist Minister named Gary Hambright, who was indicted but not convicted. These kids claimed that the people who molested them were part of a "devil worship club," and were able to describe the inside of Aquino's house, where the abuse was said to have taken place. Other children identified Aquino by his nickname, "Mikey," although Anton LaVey claims that Aquino's nickname was actually "Mickey" because his peculiar haircut made him look like Mickey Mouse (yet another Disney connection.) Although Aquino was never indicted, and the charges against Hambright were dropped, several of the children contracted STDs, proving that someone had abused them. Later, after Hambright died of AIDS, the U.S. Army wrote to the children's parents urging them to get their children tested for HIV. They also paid a multi-million-dollar settlement to the victims. Furthermore, Aquino was "Titled" by the U.S. Army for "indecent acts with a child, sodomy, conspiracy, kidnapping, and false swearing," which means that they had probable cause to believe the offenses had been committed.

According to many, the incident at Presidio was an outgrowth of Project MONARCH, and these people believe Aquino to be integrally involved in the program. Paul Bonacci has identified Aquino as the one who ordered the kidnapping of Johnny Gosch, and says that Aquino had a "ranch" in Colorado that was a "safe house" for kidnapped children. Rusty Nelson, a photographer for the Franklin Cover-Up's Lawrence King, and a convicted child pornographer, testified before a U.S. District Court on February 5, 1999 that he witnessed a suitcase full of cash being handed over to by King to Aquino that was "earmarked for the Nicaraguan Contras." Also, a number of mind-controlled sex slaves, including Cathy O'Brien, have listed Aquino as one of their "handlers." However, when I questioned Aquino about these allegations, he responded: "Throughout my entire career as an Army officer (1968-94), I never encountered any evidence of anything named or resembling 'Project MONARCH', never participated in anything involving children [or adult] 'sex slaves', never abused any children under any circumstances whatever, and never had any contact with any of the cranks who've thrown my name around with 'MONARCH.'"

The charges against Aquino perhaps lose credibility when we consider that many of the people who have made these claims have also implicated a so-called "Michael LaVey," who they say is a son of Anton LaVey. Noreen Gosch says that Michael LaVey was interviewed on a 20/20 special about her son's kidnapping, during which, according to her, "[Michael] LaVey said that he had been with Johnny on many occasions at the Satanic ritual ceremonies, where they serviced different men for their owners." Unfortunately for Noreen, no independent confirmation has surfaced that Anton had any son by that name. The late Anton LaVey himself has been implicated as a Project MONARCH participant by a handful of people, such as Noreen Gosch, but not in any specific way. However, it is interesting to note that Anton LaVey did consider Disneyland to be one of the happiest places on

Earth, and his daughter Zeena LaVey listed the 1950s thriller *The Most Dangerous Game* as her favorite movie.

The process of deprogramming a presumed victim of Project MONARCH--identifiable by abnormally wide eyes (from the electroshock), odd-looking facial moles (caused by stun guns), a plastic smile, and generally robotic behavior--is a strange and controversial one. Since slaves are programmed to self-destruct if they should ever find themselves talking about their memories, therapists wishing to override these programs must be armed with the corresponding "deactivation codes." Mark Phillips, who "rescued" Cathy O'Brien from mind control, and co-authored *The TRANCE Formation of America*, describes the process of deprogramming her: "I had to know certain codes, keys and triggers. I *had* to, and I was provided a few of those," by he says, covert communications from friends in the intelligence community. Thereafter, Cathy began to recover memories through extensive journal-writing practices. Brice Taylor used a collage method with pictures cut out of magazines.

Others use the more dubious methods of hypnosis, and similar New Age techniques to unlock memories supposedly repressed with programmed amnesia. Ritual trauma hypno-therapists such as D.C. Hammond, PhD., and Pamela J. Monday, PhD report discovering complex, multi-layered systems of programming that even take geometric shapes, such as pentagrams, hexagrams, or the cabalistic Tree of Life, complete with internal "landscapes" that have "mountains," "castles," and the like. They have found that some programs are guarded by "gatekeepers" with gothic, diabolical-sounding names, and different letters of programming are coded with letters from the Greek alphabet. For instance, Alpha is general programming, Beta involves sexual programming, Delta programming holds instructions for how to kill during ceremonies, Theta includes "psychic killing," and Omega involves suicidal, "self-destruct" programming, as well as self-mutilation. Zeta programming is related to the production of snuff films, and Omicron has to do with drug smuggling.

However, many mental health professionals cast doubt on the techniques used by hypno-therapists, charging that such practices create rather than recover memories, and so do the people who are accused of such heinous crimes on the evidence of the alleged victim's "recovered memories." The accused are backed by an organization called The False Memory Syndrome Foundation, whose spokesperson, Pamela Freyd, questions the motives of those who are, "using hypnosis, guided imagery, sodium amytal, relaxation exercise, participation in groups, reading suggestive literature and other techniques in an effort to excavate memories," Freyd explains. "Although people may remember things with any of these techniques, there is absolutely no evidence that what they remember is historically accurate." She also questions the validity of multiple personalities in general, stating that, "Many in the psychiatric community believe that MPD is iatrogenic, that is, caused by the use of hypnosis and the type of interviewing techniques of the doctor."

Confirming the validity of another person's memory is nearly impossible, especially if every other person involved in the memory denies that it took place. However, it may perhaps be unfair to label as "impossible" or "ridiculous" the memories of other people which merely lie beyond the spectrum of our own experience. Many of us received religious indoctrination from our family as we grew up, and were forced to participate in weird ceremonies that made us uncomfortable. Isn't it logical that if our parents were Satanists or occultists, they might subject us to similar indoctrination? And since Satanic and occult practices purportedly bestow worldly power upon their practitioners, isn't it logical that some of our most powerful leaders might participate in such practices? Isn't it logical that they would make use of occult-based mind control techniques such as hypnotism, rituals, mind-altering drugs, and Neuro-Linguistic Programming (i.e., rote memorization of "magic words")--techniques that have been traditional components of religious ceremonies, from the mystical priesthoods of Babylon, Greece, Rome and Egypt to the "cults" of today?

The CIA's interest in mind control is well-documented, and there was certainly a time, in which they had no compunction about subjecting unwitting subjects to experiments that might harm them, or which might go against their intended will. The idea that the CIA would traffic in guns, drugs and other contraband in order to fund their secret projects is becoming more generally accepted, especially after *The San Francisco Chronicle*'s Gary Webb investigated the funding of Contra aid in 1996.

Furthermore, we know that men in positions of power often require a greater-than-average number of sexual partners, often choosing extremely young women (or men), sometimes prostitutes, to satisfy their often kinky desires. Perhaps this is just a result of the greater-than-average testosterone levels often found in aggressive power-seekers. That the CIA would supply these prostitutes in exchange for their much-needed Black Ops funding, and that they would keep these prostitutes mind-controlled into silence using the above-mentioned techniques, so as to cover their own tracks, may not be impossible to believe.

Perhaps what people do find unbelievable is the sheer sensationalism of so many of the "Project MONARCH" stories. The mental picture of George Bush, Sr. sodomizing a seven-year-old boy, or of Bill Clinton participating in cannibalistic baby sacrifice, is not one that most people can take seriously. Even more difficult to overcome, perhaps, is a natural disbelief that arises when a person claiming to have been under complete mental robotism, and subjected to unimaginable torture throughout his or her entire life appears to "recover" so quickly after the "memories" are revealed during therapy. Some of them even go on to write books, conduct seminars, and make radio appearances, becoming a professional victim-expert. Perhaps we will never know who is and who isn't telling the truth about MONARCH mind control--unless the documents that supposedly exist are one day declassified. However, the tales of Project MONARCH provide an interesting framework in which to interpret current events, especially the never-ending sex scandals that perpetually crop up amongst our public figures.

Bibliography

De Camp, John, *The Franklin Cover-Up*, AWT, 1992, USA.

O'Brien, Cathy, and Phillips, Mark, *The TRANCE Formation of America*, Reality Marketing, 1995, USA

McKenna, Annie, *Paperclip Dolls: MK-ULTRA, Mind Control, and Project PAPERCLIP, 1999, USA.*

Springmeier, Fritz, *Bloodlines of the Illuminati,* Ambassador House, 1998, USA.

Taylor, Brice, *Thanks for the Memories... The Truth Has Set Me Free: The Memoirs of Bob Hope's and Henry Kissinger's Mind-Controlled Slave*, Brice Taylor Trust. 1999.

The preceding is the lengthier version of an article originally written in late 2001. A shorter, edited version of it was published in the December 2002 issue of *Hustler Magazine*. The following interviews were conducted as part of the research for this article.

The Most Dangerous Game:
An Interview with Cathy O'Brien

By Tracy R. Twyman

Cathy O'Brien is the author, with her husband Mark Phillips, of *The TRANCE Formation of America*, and *ACCESS DENIED For Reasons of National Security.* She says that she and her daughter Kelly were used for years as mind-controlled sex slaves for the CIA. Her husband is Mark Phillips, who, they claim, rescued her and her daughter from this life of abuse and deprogrammed Cathy's mind control conditioning. For years they have been on a crusade to educate the public about secret government mind control programs. This interview took place in October of 2001.

TRACY: At what age did you begin to be sexually abused?

CATHY: I was sexually abused as far back as I can remember, and I recall my father saying that he had abused me since infancy, substituting his penis for my mother's nipple.

TRACY: Who did he say this to?

CATHY: He said this to quite a few people who were involved in incest, which was real prominent in the area of Muskegon, Michigan, where I grew up. It was a common point of conversation, and was what I thought was the normal way people lived.

TRACY: So everyone in the town was doing it, and talking about it?

CATHY: Well, I don't know about everyone, but everyone in my environment seemed to be involved in it, and since then Muskegon has been named as a pedophile capitol. Even the *Muskegon Chronicle* said that [Muskegon was] the primary place in the United States for pedophiles, so there was an extensive exposé on that. But the area where I grew up in was definitely predominantly full of incest and sexual abuse.

TRACY: So do you think that this had been going on for generations in that area? Is it just, like, a culture that developed over there?

CATHY: I'm not really sure exactly how it happened, but I do know that Project PAPERCLIP had brought over Nazi scientists that had learned that multi-generational incest-based families would have children that were sexually abused, which would result in a dissociative disorder that was a prime basis for mind control. So they were really interested in that aspect of things. And in Muskegon, the local politicians were actually sanctioning that type of activity, where there wasn't any prosecution of the pedophiles in the court system, like my father. He actually received immunity from prosecution for using me in child pornography. The deal was that he would raise me according to the government specifications, which were based on the Hitler/Himmler research into the multi-generational incest children. So it was widely spread, widely known, and actually a deliberate effort that was going on in the Muskegon area at that time.

TRACY: So when did the mind control programming start for you? At what age?

CATHY: The mind control aspect began when I was about 6 years old, which was in the early 1960s, when the local politicians were sanctioning the local Michigan mafia child pornography rings, because they knew that any child that was sexually abused to that extent would be suffering from this dissociative disorder that they were interested in targeting for mind control. So they were trying to locate children like myself. And they found some child pornography that had been made, and my father was approached at that time by a criminal faction of our government that was interested in the proliferation of mind control, and told that he would receive immunity from prosecution if he would sell me into the project. So he did, and I was six years old at the time. So mind control conditioning began from a very, very early age.

TRACY: And who is this "criminal faction of the government." Is there a name for them?

CATHY: I don't know of a name, per se, for them, but the more people learn about mind control, and the more they research what mind control entails, how it's being used in various aspects of our society, like the military, and Special Forces, and levels of espionage in the capacity that I was used on the CIA's MK-ULTRA mind control during the Reagan/Bush administration--the more people know, the more they're going to be able to recognize who these perpetrators are, and what kind of controls they actually inflict, not only on individuals like myself, but also in a mass mind control aspect that was also taken from the Nazi Germany Hitler/Himmler research.

TRACY: A lot of people in the conspiracy theory field have a name for this group of people. They call them the Illuminati. People imagine them as being a secret society, or a cabal of organized people, and I was just wondering if you'd ever heard a term like that.

CATHY: I've heard various terms, but people participated in different secret organizations, and I think that's the key to where the problem lies, is in the secrecy. People have a right to this information, they need to know this information, and it's imperative that the facts regarding mind control be brought to light, and taken out of these secret societies. Things aren't so easily black and white. I can't just point a finger at one particular faction, or one particular group, because there's good and bad in everything, including the CIA. Not all CIA's bad. Not all government's bad, you know. It's just not that simple.

TRACY: When did you first hear the term "Project MONARCH," and associate that with what was happening to you?

CATHY: When I was about 9 years old was when I first heard that term, and at that time I was being routinely taken to the Governor's Mansion in Mackinaw Island, Michigan.

TRACY: Who was the governor at that time?

CATHY: The Governor was George Romney. That's when I was really being conditioned, and thrust into a more government level of mind control. He's not a main perpetrator. He was one that was actively involved in mind control in the educational system and everything. Names of course are in our book *The TRANCE Formation of America*, but my focus is more on just the mind control information rather than who the perpetrators are, because if people find out what the components of mind control are, they're going to be able to identify these people, and that's going to put us a lot further ahead, rather than information of who was involved back in the early 60s. But, nevertheless, that was the first time I heard the term "Project MONARCH," and I heard it at various times. Of course, I had no capacity to really understand that, aside from the fact that I knew that it was widespread.

TRACY: What were the methods used when you were a child to program your mind?

CATHY: I had a dissociative disorder, which is professionally defined as "the mind's sane defense against trauma too horrible to comprehend," and of course sexual abuse is too horrible to comprehend for a child. There's no place for that in the brain. The brain actually compartmentalizes the memory of that event so that the mind can function normally. So I had these dissociative barriers set up in my brain, which was already prime for conditioning, for programming, and for them to be able to put into my highly suggestible mind, a conditioning and information that they wanted in there for a base of future programming. So from the very outset, my whole environment was controlled. For example, my TV was controlled, what I read was controlled, and absolutely my music was controlled, because of the harmonic effects on the brain. The news that I received was all controlled. So having my environment controlled to that extent about what went in my brain, my knowledge base was actually formed according to what they wanted. We all form opinions, fact, and ultimately our actions based on what we know. And what we need to know is that there has been alternate knowledge that doesn't fit in a box, and we have got to learn to think further, and think beyond just what we have been told, and begin to look further and ask questions. Asking questions was something that I wasn't capable of under mind control. I could only accept information, only take it in. I had no ability to creatively use it, to think to use that information, but nevertheless it was pumped into my head at a rate that created what is termed "artificial intelligence" by some. It's a form of artificial intelligence that's actually pumped into the mind, because the brain accepts the information on a photographic level when trauma like incest occurs. These are the kind of facts that the Hitler/Himmler research had discovered, and was actually being built from and expanded on during my earliest years, in the course of bringing MK-ULTRA mind control so heavily into our society.

TRACY: I've heard this described many times by "survivors" of this, who say that there were levels of programming with Greek letter codes, like Alpha and Beta and Delta. Did that happen to you?

CATHY: That is something that I am ever so vaguely familiar with, but that would be a good question to talk to Mark about, because that is definitely not my area. That's more outside information rather than what I would know from the inside.

TRACY: You said that they controlled the music you heard. What did they want you to listen to?

CATHY: There was a lot of music going on back in those days that I have missed and have only found since I have been recovered and deprogrammed and have been able to choose music for myself. But the 60s freedom music I didn't get to listen to, and any kind of protest, or anything like that. Instead I had to listen to country music. That ultimately was the industry that I traveled in during the Reagan/Bush administration, under the control primarily of Senator Byrd, who was my owner in MK-ULTRA.

TRACY: When did Senator Byrd become your controller? And what was he like back then? Because now he's sort of a doddering old man. He's always shaking. Was he like that when you knew him.

CATHY: No. I've been familiar with him all my life, or all of my mind-controlled existence rather. Because there's not any "life" under mind control per se, because there's no capacity for free thought, no capacity for free will, or ultimately any soul expression. So I could only robotically do the things that I was told to do, and during those years I was exposed to numerous high-profile political perpetrators that were involved in MK-ULTRA. They are, of course, named in our book, *The TRANCE Formation of America*.

TRACY: What was the progression of controllers that you had. Was there more than one at a time?

CATHY: I had what is termed "handlers," and handlers would make sure that I was in various places at certain times, either on military or NASA installations for mind control programming, or in and out of Washington, D.C. I traveled under the guise of the country music industry, because it provided a means of travel in and out of the Caribbean, Mexico, and Canada, which were primarily the areas I was used in, as well as all across the United States. So my handler would make sure that I was in designated areas at specific times, either for programming, or to carry out the covert operations that I was used in during the Reagan/Bush administration.

TRACY: OK, so Senator Byrd was not the only one. Is there a difference between a handler and an owner, or a controller?

CATHY: I had two different handlers in the course of being under absolute robotic mind control, and my father, I'm sure, would be considered a handler as well, because once he agreed to raise me according to government specifications, he followed their instructions and followed what they told him to do with me, and where to take me, how to condition me, how to control my environment, and things like that. So in essence, he was my first handler. When MK-ULTRA came into my life, the regimentation, the systematic kind of conditioning and abuse and programming that I received from that point on was far more structured than the natural high suggestibility resultant from the incest and the pornography that I was used in as a very young child. My father was approached and told. He didn't think to do this on his own, in other words. He was being told. So he became a handler. Handlers follow instructions. Owners are the ones who decide which projects or which operations to use someone in, and in my case, that was Senator Byrd, and that was how I ended up on a higher government level. I first met him at Mackinaw Island, at the Governor's mansion when I was 13 years old, and that's when he became my owner, which lasted throughout my victimization right up until Mark rescued me and my daughter in 1988.

TRACY: As far as the operations that you were used in for Project MONARCH--it started out with prostitution and pornography, right?

CATHY: Right.

TRACY: And then did it move into other areas? Were you used as a drug mule?

CATHY: Well, I think the next step that was so significant to me was the use of occultism. At that time the local Catholic church-- and again, I'm not saying that all Catholics are involved and that they're all bad, but there is a criminal faction within the Catholic Church, within the Order of the Jesuits, which is the intelligence arm of the Vatican, a part of which my family ultimately had ties into and was a further causation for me to be victimized within the church system. But nevertheless, the Catholic Church was heavily involved in the sexual abuse of children, which was widespread and has definitely come to light. They've had to pay out on numerous child abuse cases as a result. But the reversal of the Catholic Mass is, of course, Satanism, and being exposed to Satanism is definitely trauma too horrible to comprehend. Any kind of blood trauma like that is really horrible, and that was used to further dissociate my mind, further compartmentalize it for future programming. And that theme was used right through my second handler. Well, really, right on through my whole victimization there was always some aspect of occultism that came in as well. And alien themes were also a very common trauma base. Anything that's beyond our ability to affect or control, or something in our minds that we perceive as too big to be able to affect like that is what they would use to ultimately gain control. Superstition begins where knowledge leaves off, and superstition makes a person more suggestible and easily controlled, so they definitely used superstitious kind of themes to further program.

Those were significant trauma bases.

TRACY: Yeah, I understand from your book that there were Satanic rituals that took place at this Catholic church. Were there Satanic rituals that took place elsewhere throughout your life?

CATHY: Definitely, and so often they're done more as a trauma base for mind control. It's even used in the military which, for example, has the occult Temple of Set, which is supposedly more intellectually based, which is used to traumatize people. That leaves them widely suggestible for mind control programming. It's a very deliberate method, and it has proliferated heavily on our military bases. And it was certainly a part of my victimization right up until Mark rescued my daughter and me. And I say "rescued" because I had lost my ability to even think to survive. There was nothing I could do to pull us out of our situation. I couldn't think about what was happening. I was so robotic by that time. It took someone with eyes to see and ears to hear, and a heart to care to be able to take us out of the situation that we were in.

TRACY: You seem to be saying that these people were not religiously Satanists. They were just using it to control people.

CATHY: Oftentimes that was the case.

TRACY: But do you think there is a spiritual aspect to this, where they actually believe in the power of Satan, or of these other gods?

CATHY: I think there are some that believe that, but the primary mind control programmers who use that for a theme certainly know better and know that the so-called "Satanic power" was in the form of a stun gun and sophisticated mind control programming [methodologies] that included harmonics, and a deliberate, systematic use of sleep, food, and water deprivation. That was what they really knew to be the ultimate power, and didn't have anything to do with anything spiritual.

TRACY: There was, in your programming, a lot of imagery from Disney and other popular children's movies which was used. And also there was something you were forced to participate in called

"The Most Dangerous Game." Have you seen that movie, *The Most Dangerous Game*?

CATHY: No.

TRACY: It's this movie from the 50s about human hunting.

CATHY: I wonder if that was based on the military maneuver, or if the military maneuver sprang from it. I'm not familiar with that movie, but I am familiar with the military maneuver of playing "The Most Dangerous Game," where a person is in the woods and attempting to survive while they're being hunted. That was the kind of trauma that I was exposed to for programming purposes.

TRACY: I thought that it was significant when I found this out the other day: one of Anton LaVey's favorite places in the world was Disneyland, and his daughter, Zeena LaVey's favorite movie was *The Most Dangerous Game*.

CATHY: I think one of the strongest weapons is a scramble of fantasy and reality, kind of along the same lines as military programming tactics. They use a video game for military training, and they can't tell reality from the video, so when they're actually in a combat situation, it's more like they're just playing out a video game. They lose their ability to consciously comprehend what they're doing, and to be able to critically analyze it, which is really essential. And so they end up just being able to point and shoot, point and shoot, without giving it any real thought to the magnitude of what's actually happening. They'll play it out more like a video game. And oftentimes with mind control programming, they would attempt to scramble it with a movie, hence the conditioning of the Disney movies and all, which were quite extensively used. But the primary one which was used was *The Wizard of Oz*, because of the kind of dimensional aspects that come into play of "over the rainbow." We see a lot of indications that this is still going on today.

TRACY: Do you think that the movies were written and edited specifically for the use of mind control, or was the mind control adapted to the movies?

CATHY: That's a good question, and I wouldn't really know.

TRACY: When your father started participating in Project MONARCH, didn't you say that Gerald Ford came over to the house to give him instructions?

CATHY: Well, he was a local politician, and as his career escalated, so too did my victimization. But then, again, I don't know how you want to go about naming names and the best way to put it in this particular article, so I'll leave it up to you and your discretion. But ultimately for names, I think I'd refer them to the book, because *The TRANCE Formation of America* was written for the U.S. Congressional Select Committee on Intelligence Oversight, and the facts that are in the book are all well-documented, where they would be able to have a point of reference for understanding exactly the material that was written there, probably more so than the average person on the street. So the documentation, the absolute facts, and names are definitely in the book.

TRACY: So you don't want to talk about the specific people that were involved, is that what you're saying?

CATHY: I think that I would much rather be able to put out information on mind control, and the people involved in it, and the reality of it, and how widespread it is, so that people would be able to arm themselves with the knowledge and actually evolve with this knowledge, because knowledge is our only defense against mind control. And right now, at this point in time, it's essential that people have this information, because it's a key component of what's terrorizing America and the world today. Terrorism breeds mind control. Mind control breeds terror, and people have got to have the information on mind control now more than ever. It will be able to stop the sexual abuse of children, the injustice in the courts that is perpetrated on the children, and there is so much that we're going to be able to do when we have the information. I'm afraid it would even sidetrack people to say, "This person, that person is involved, or was involved then," when they can be seeing today who's involved based on a strong knowledge of mind control.

Going back to one other aspect, which personally I think is so very, very important, is the use of Satanism and everything like that, because they can't control a soul per se. When a mind is absolutely controlled, there's no free thought, and if there's no free thought, there's no free will. And without free will, there's no ability to have any soul expression. If a person doesn't have soul expression, they can't stand up for what they believe in, they can't stand up for a cause, they can't stand up for moral values, or anything like that, which I consider to be more related to soul. So it's not that they can control the soul, but by controlling the mind, they stop the person from being able to express it. I think that shows the magnitude of mind control, and how very important it is that people know that our knowledge base is being altered, that this information is being suppressed, and people are being led and misled by a deliberate use of a form of mass mind control, which is also called "social engineering."

TRACY: How would you identify someone who was actually being purposely controlled to the point where they're almost a robot. Is there some kind of telltale sign? Can you tell if someone's a mind-controlled slave just by looking at them, or seeing the way they act?

CATHY: I can tell it just from having been there and experienced it, and seeing how widespread it is and where it's used and everything. I've learned to recognize certain characteristics or traits of mind control. For example, people under mind control rarely blink. Their eyes stay wide open. And the micro-muscles in their face don't move properly, so they don't have proper facial expression. They may always smile. I smiled, I think, the whole time that I was under mind control. I had a little plastic smile plastered on my face. My face looked waxy otherwise, and there was no smile in my eyes, there was no twinkle, no depth to that little smile. There are certain mannerisms that can be recognized. There's a more rigid stance, or something that might be equated more to a militaristic stance.

TRACY: It seems like if you were to go to a modeling school, this is what they're trying to teach those women to do.

CATHY: That's what Charm School did, and everybody that I was associated with back then was being programmed alongside of me. It was like they were cranking us out so that we'd pretty much look the same. You know, people that are conditioned the same way do seem to have a certain look, or certain mannerisms about them. Politicians have a way of looking a certain way. I'm not saying that they're programmed. It's just their knowledge base and the way they're conditioned. Attorneys might have a way that they talk, and a way that they're conditioned. You know, people have different projections, and folks that have been conditioned for mind control definitely have an identifiable projection that people need to know now more than ever. We're being told that it's up to us to stay alert, and on guard, and watch out for potential terrorists, anyone who's acting or looking suspicious. Well, that's not enough information. They need to release the information on mind control so that people will know exactly what to look for, exactly what characteristics and traits to be watching for. The more people know, the better off we're all going to be in this effort to stop terrorism. I've got some insight into what mind control looks like.

I've got insight into some of the old characteristics. For instance, the stun gun was one used so predominantly, and a stun gun leaves electric prod marks that are two inches apart. It will actually leave moles, or raised places that turn into moles eventually. They're oftentimes located on the face, and those are so easily identifiable. I see people all the time on TV, especially in pornography magazines, that have these stun gun prod marks on them. And when we become aware of exactly what these stun gun prod marks mean, that opens our eyes to being able to recognize mind control around us as well. I think that's another essential part. But stun guns aren't used as much today because they've moved technologically ahead with harmonics and different aspects now. Stun guns are still used, and the prod marks still show up on many people who were conditioned, particularly during the years I was used robotically under MK-ULTRA.

TRACY: Well, they used one on JonBenet Ramsey, didn't they? I remember the story coming out in *The Enquirer*, where they finally looked at the autopsy pictures, and they found these stun gun marks, two inches apart, just like you said, on her body.

CATHY: That's why this information is so essential. The more people know, the more they're going to be able to ask questions, and they're going to start seeing it in society all around them, and in these murders, and deaths, and terror and different aspects that come in to play, they're going to be able to say, "Oh that's what that is!," and they're going to start recognizing it. They're going to start noticing it in the music industry. It's used heavily in the music industry, and certain high-level entertainers have been subjected to it. There are lawsuits that have gone on because certain entertainers are given the harmonic equipment to use in their music, which drives their lyrics further into a person's head. If you think about it, people know that a song will bring them back to a time when they fell in love, for example, or a time when they were doing this, or doing that. Songs bring out memories because of how deep the harmonics carry into the brain. That has been fine-tuned and refined so much now that it is an essential tool. If the information on mind control were now released, people would realize that is what is causing people to take action with the lyrics that are going in their head. That's what's causing them to react, and carry out a murder based on having listened to this music or that.

It's not about free speech, and it's not about the lyrics. It's about harmonics, and that is one more key ingredient, and one more aspect of society where people need to become aware of exactly what mind control entails. Once they're aware of it, they can critically analyze and defend themselves against it, as well as recognize it around them so that we know what a terrorist looks like, what mind control looks like, and who's being abused, what's the devastation that sexual abuse ultimately creates, in raising suggestibility, and how people are being manipulated, even on a mass scale, through trauma. Any time trauma occurs, suggestibility rises. So when we have trauma, like we've got now, with this horrible terror that occurred in the United States, people everywhere are so highly suggestible at a time like this, they need to be on guard about what information is being pumped into their heads, especially if it's repetitive. They need to shut off their TVs, they need to think for themselves, and there are different methods they can use to be able to refocus themselves, and maintain their own freedom of thought at a time when the most extensive trauma occurs. So with this information, people are actually able to strengthen, and be far more vigilant. One of our last remaining freedoms is free thought.

TRACY: You said in your book that part of your programming was decorating your room in red, white and blue, with American flags. Is it getting to you now that everyone has a flag?

CATHY: Well, absolutely, I was very patriotic, and I think patriotism is one thing that's separating people from each other. This isn't about that. Terrorism isn't about countries. This is about individuals. This is a mind control issue, not a country issue, so if folks want to find strength in waving a flag, it's because they don't know the essential point and focus of what's really happening, and that's mind control. And once they realize that, then we're not going to have to take the strong divisions, either by race, country, religion, or anything else, but people can unite in peace and through love, rather than having to fight the so-called "enemy" of another country. That really isn't what this is about at all. So again, this is such an essential ingredient to what's happening in society today. Patriotism certainly isn't the answer. It's quite superficial. If people would just turn off their TVs, they'd be able to find a lot more answers than they would by going out and buying a flag.

TRACY: But hasn't it gotten to you that when President Bush and others talk about this war coming on, they refer to it in international terms, and they want everyone in the world to join in this fight against terrorism? Doesn't it seem like the ultimate end of this could be a one-world government?

CATHY: Well, ultimately, people aren't going to wake up in time, because this was such an enormous trauma that absolutely has shaken people to their knees. It's my fervent hope that we can be able to get information out through folks like yourself who are writing articles, and through every possible public means to get the information out on mind control so that people are going to be able to make a positive difference in time to stop this effort. You've got a situation where criminal activity has perpetuated to this point. The tons of covert activities that I was used in during the

Reagan/Bush administration included the CIA's covert operation of the drug industry. And the drugs, of course, were cocaine, primarily, as well as heroin. The poppy fields in Afghanistan were certainly a part of my victimization, and in our book, *The TRANCE Formation of America* it's mentioned as well. But the whole Iran-Contra thing feeds into it. At one time we were funding the war against the Soviet Union so that the Soviet Union would topple, because they were the Evil Empire at the time. And now all of the sudden we've got terrorists that have resulted from it. The negativity just continues to breed.

It's very, very much like what's happening in the military where they found out only 15% of the people could shoot their so-called "enemy," they didn't figure that number was high enough. They had to bypass critical analysis, and the way to do that was to get people to not think, just to do it. Point and shoot, point and shoot, without any thought or critical analysis of the fact that they were killing another person. The best way to do that was to condition them through video games, the same video games that our children are playing. I mean, they're playing with a very, very dangerous weapon in itself that's teaching them to bypass critical analysis. What happens then is that programming goes into place, where the military will point and shoot, point and shoot. And then they leave the military, they're turned out onto the streets, without being deprogrammed. It's turning our streets into a bloodbath, it's creating extreme violence, and the children are being conditioned into violence that we're seeing coming out now in the school systems. Because they're being conditioned in exactly the same way, to take away that critical analysis. The whole negative aspect of everything is ultimately what is coming out onto us now through this terrorism, and when we realize what the cause is, and can be able to think for ourselves and critically analyze once again what's really going on, we're going to realize that war and fighting is not the answer. Then people will unite through natural attrition. They'll unite with cause. They'll unite with peace and love. Ultimately, that's the kind of world unity that I would like to see. The only way that we can achieve that is by getting the information out on the reality of mind control, because this is absolutely a case where the truth makes us free.

TRACY: [Getting back to your childhood], how did you function in school while all of this was happening to you?

CATHY: I got very high grades in school. Mostly As, because when trauma occurs that's too horrible to comprehend, the brain automatically goes into its own mode, and it photographically records events surrounding the trauma. For example, most people know exactly where and what they were doing when Kennedy was assassinated. That's an example from that time when I was growing up that I think most people would be able to relate to, and that's an example of how the brain photographically records events surrounding trauma. Since I was being traumatized all the time, I was photographically recording what I was being taught in school. So I got excellent grades. I wasn't able to use that information, but I was still receiving the information. It was still being driven into my brain.

TRACY: So after you graduated high school, did you go on to higher education? Did you have a career?

CATHY: I had a couple of years of college just as I was being thrust totally into MK-ULTRA. When I was 18, of legal age, I was transferred to Louisiana, where I endured extreme occult trauma for a period of three years, which left me so primed for mind control that it was during those three years that I became absolutely robotic, and began being used on a government level. So, from about the time I was 18 years old on, I was used in government operations. But prior to that I went through education as far as I could, and that included several semesters of junior college.

TRACY: Did you have career goals in mind? And since the government was using you, were they also providing for you financially? Did you have a job?

CATHY: No, I wasn't provided for financially. I worked different jobs, like most teens would, but I was working three jobs at the time, just menial jobs, plus going to school. And what this did was it kept me wore down. Sleep deprivation was necessary for the kind of conditioning that I was going through at that time.

TRACY: And when you talk about "severe occult trauma," were there human sacrifices involved?

CATHY: Yes.

TRACY: Were you forced to participate in that?

CATHY: Was forced to see it, not participate, per se. It was a trauma base for me.

TRACY: And is Kelly your only child, as far as you know?

CATHY: Yes.

TRACY: Did they, while they were abusing you, have you on birth control?

CATHY: Oh yeah. Predominantly, yeah, but first I had Kelly. I had her during the years that I was being traumatized so horrifically with the occultism. Kelly was born into MK-ULTRA on a much more sophisticated level than I had been exposed to. She was conditioned literally from birth, and on a harmonics, high-tech level, whereas mine had been on a sexual abuse and trauma level. And that initial upbringing that I had was the kind of mind control that I was maintained under throughout my victimization, whereas my daughter Kelly was almost immediately thrust into the harmonic level. I couldn't think to save her from it any more than I could think to save myself, and we could only do exactly what we were told to do, both of us.

TRACY: Now, when she was being programmed, would they take her away from you?

CATHY: Oftentimes, and sometimes not. It depends on the trauma base. Often multi-generational incest-based families will have children who are sexually abuse, who sexually abuse their children, and so it goes. Both my father and my brother were sexually abused, so they sexually abused me. In my case, for whatever reason, that gene didn't come through to me. I can't comprehend pedophilia. I cannot comprehend the sexual abuse of a child. Despite my whole upbringing, having been in it, for me to think of sexually abusing a child is just

--I don't know why people would even want to do that, and I'm certainly not into the control thing either. My daughter's abuse was used against me to traumatize me. Of all the tortures, of all the traumas, of all the horrors that I saw and witnessed and experienced throughout my victimization, any abuse, including sexual abuse, of my daughter was the most horrible, horrible thing that I ever endured. It was absolutely awful.

TRACY: So they never forced you to participate in it?

CATHY: There were different situations that I was forced into with Kelly. For example, I was used in pornography throughout my victimization, from the time I was a little bitty child right on through. But most of the kind of sexual filming that was done was covert filming that was used for blackmail purposes. In cases like that, I am aware of several instances where my daughter was present, and that is truly the most horrible thing that I've ever experienced, and I've experienced a lot of awful things. But nevertheless, that was used.

TRACY: Was Kelly ever taken to Bohemian Grove?

CATHY: Yes. We both have been there.

TRACY: Is that like a big Satanic group meeting for people in positions of power?

CATHY: Again, this is where we separate the superstition from the hard-core facts. They would use that theme perhaps for traumatization, but it was not the leading theme, or the predominant theme whenever we were at the Grove. When we were taken to the Grove, it was usually a meeting of global leaders that were actively involved in the New World Order effort through mind control of the masses. They had the same agenda, they were like minds, and they would come together in a place like Bohemian Grove to meet and discuss their plans, and actually formulate them. The worst things I heard there had to do with mass genocide rather than occultism.

TRACY: So when they're having these meetings, and they're talking about New World Order policy, are those meetings separate from all the kinky sex that goes on there? Is that recreation that takes place after the meetings?

CATHY: Well, it's secretive there, and it's my experience that when these people got together, they didn't have, like, a formal round table sit-down with ties and suits, for Heaven's sakes. You know, this was very informal, and they would just talk as friends talk. Because they felt that they were in an environment that wasn't being monitored, and wasn't being scrutinized by anyone, they felt free to do whatever they wanted. That certainly went into areas of perversion, and a lot of cocaine use, and whatever they were wanting to indulge in, they felt free to do.

TRACY: Have you seen Stanley Kubrick's *Eyes Wide Shut*?

CATHY: Yeah, I have.

TRACY: Was that an accurate representation of one of these experiences at Bohemian Grove?

CATHY: You know, I think the theme was taken from that, but I can't really relate to it. It's not quite the same. But there are aspects of it that are probably more realistic than any other occult movie that I'm familiar with.

TRACY: They have the Cremation of Care ceremony (at Bohemian Grove), in which some people have accused them of sacrificing babies, by tossing them into a huge bonfire in front of a giant owl statue. But the official story from Bohemian Grove is that they're actually tossing bundles of stick into the bonfire. Is that correct?

CATHY: Yeah, but that wasn't a primary aspect of my victimization. It was part of a threat that whatever I did I had to do as though my life depended on it, because it did. And I've certainly seen people die. The secretiveness of the Grove and what went on there would certainly lend itself to that kind of trauma.

TRACY: Have you ever seen babies sacrificed?

CATHY: During the horrible conditioning of those three years that I mentioned, yes.

TRACY: I've heard of "Mother Goddesses" who are used as breeders for these babies. Have you ever met anyone like that?

CATHY: No, actually, that goes into, I think, the more superstitious aspect of the occult, rather than the deliberate use of occultism for a trauma base for mind control. The level I was used on was a White House/Pentagon level, so it was pretty extreme, pretty regimented, whereas I think what you're talking about there is a little more New Agey, a little more along those lines. So I'm not as familiar with that. I'm more familiar with genetic studies in breeding that were going on for genetic purposes, and genetic mind control. That's what Project MONARCH is: it's a genetic mind control project, and it's part of MK-ULTRA. MK-ULTRA has different branches, and the one that I was subjected to was a genetic mind control project. So I'm more familiar with things from that end than I am from the aspect you mentioned. Like in my daughter's case, she was born for espionage. Her father was mind-controlled, and he was used in mercenary paramilitary operations in very murderous aspects. They wanted to breed those abilities in with mine, which were more on a message-delivering aspect and a sexual aspect. And so they combined two multi-generational mind control slaves for creating Kelly. That's all I know. That's the kind of thing that I was exposed to, was that kind of deliberate effort. I certainly wouldn't have chosen to have anything to do with Wayne Cox under any circumstances, especially to father my child.

TRACY: So you were used as kind of a storage server for information, and a courier, correct?

CATHY: Very much so, and used primarily in the drug industry. The cocaine operations were so heavy back in those days, in the Caribbean and Mexico. I was used on the groundwork of NAFTA with then-President De la Madrid and Vice-President Salinas, and it had been determined even back then, when I was being used, that Salinas was going to go into the office of President of Mexico when George Bush went into the office of President of the United States. So it was already pre-determined. Both of them were in the Vice-Presidential capacity, and yet both of them had more power and influence than the figurehead presidents of both our countries. I saw some extreme inner workings in the groundwork for NAFTA. I was used in the capacity of funding the New World Order efforts [via] the CIA's involvement in the cocaine industry.

TRACY: Did you have any prior knowledge that George Bush, Jr. was going to be President?

CATHY: I knew that he was being conditioned. I had seen him. I knew he was definitely jostling for that. But I didn't know that aspect of it. I did hear conversations about Bill Clinton, but, you know, I'd refer people to the book on something like that. I wouldn't want to be quoted on that.

TRACY: Do you still believe that you have an immunity to all sexually transmitted diseases--that they gave this to you as part of your training?

CATHY: I have no reason not to believe that.

TRACY: Do you think that "They," the bad guys, have purposely bred AIDS, and other diseases like that, or have allowed them to proliferate while they possess the antidote or the vaccine.

CATHY: Mass genocide has been discussed, and has certainly come to pass and been perpetrated. AIDS is something that I have cause to suspect in that regard, based on the operations I was used for in Haiti, and based on conversations that I heard. Also, consider the fact that they did not use any kind of sexual protection whatsoever in the sexual activities that I was engaged in with these various government leaders, even coming right back from Haiti where AIDS was already rampant. Also, there was quite a bit of confidence surrounding that fact, and it was a known fact--that since I was used on a White House/Pentagon level, and was what they termed a "Presidential Model," they would not get AIDS from me, because I was "clean." That was the term used.

TRACY: Are these perpetrators primarily white and male? I know that you had experience with Hillary Clinton, and some other wives of prominent people. Do you think that there are a lot of women that are involved in this as well, on a hierarchical level?

CATHY: I knew several that were heavily involved. I think the mindset or propensity towards the New World Order effort through mind control of the masses spans all genders, race, countries, and nationalities. I don't see any differentiation except mindset, and there are people that believe the only way to world peace is through mind control of the masses. How can we have world peace that way, if there's no soul expression? That's a different definition of peace, which I guess would require peace-keeping forces rather than the power of love.

TRACY: If they're talking about mass genocide, though, then there must be certain groups of people that they wish to eliminate. I mean, did you not get that impression?

CATHY: Especially from a genetic aspect, yes, they wanted what they termed the "less desirables" to be eliminated from the planet, because the planet was what they considered to be too overpopulated anyway. I've definitely heard conversations to that effect, and the predictions that I heard I've seen come about, particularly through the spread of AIDS.

TRACY: But there are elite strains within all of the races that you are aware of that were considered worthy by them to preserve, and it's just the lower elements of all the races that they want to eliminate. Is that correct?

CATHY: I would say so to a large degree, but mostly it's the ones in the so-called "secret societies," the people who were of like mind that they considered to be the most evolved and the ones who should survive.

TRACY: Were you ever abused within the confines of a Masonic lodge?

CATHY: Oh yes. Oh yes! Even in my younger years, because my mother's father ran a Masonic lodge in Michigan. I mean, it was definitely sprinkled throughout my victimization. But then again, I wouldn't say all Masons are bad, but I don't think all Masons know what the ultimate secrets are.

TRACY: But you think this New World Order philosophy might be one of the ultimate secrets of Masonic teachings.

CATHY: I believe it's an ultimate goal of many of them that are involved in Masonic aspects. But then again, any time you've got secret societies, and information is suppressed, they operate on the philosophy that secret knowledge equals power, and if they've got secret knowledge, they can exercise it over other people. That's exactly what's been happening for way too long, and that's why I say, "It's truth that sets us free." It's time to start telling their secrets. It's time for the truth to be brought to light so that everyone can see exactly what's going on, and as far as I'm concerned, that's the only way we're going to be able to effectively combat terrorism.

TRACY: Well, the thing is that people have very short attention spans, and they don't have to be programmed to be that way. They are that way naturally. So how do you distill a message so that it's actually useful for people who hear it? I mean, if they see a "60 Minutes" piece on this, is that going to do it? Because in mind control, they distill a message down to a phrase or a couple of words, and they repeat that over and over again until people have it burned into their brains. Is there some way of distilling this information so that people will finally catch on?

CATHY: They need to expand their thoughts, and ask questions, and think outside the box. They've been limited in their thinking for so long, and it's like, people have gotten lazy mentally. It's time that we expand our thinking. When I recovered from mind control, what I had experienced was a more exaggerated scale of what everyone goes through. I mean, there is a form of mind control on a mass scale. There is a social engineering. There is a conditioning that has taken place. That, combined with the deliberate militaristic aspect, through things like video games, and stuff, is further conditioning society: the suppression of pertinent information, the suppression of technology, the suppression even of a fact like harmonics. Once people know about that, then we can be more vigilant to protect our free thought, instead of just having things driven into our heads through TV and through music. This is pertinent information. Why should it be a National Security secret? Why are the components of mind control being kept secret under the guise of National Security? It's National Security that's threatening the security of our nation, threatening the security of our free thought, and threatening the security of humanity as we know it. People have a right to this information, and it's time that it came out. When people realize that mind control is a reality, they're going to begin to ask questions. Asking questions is the key for them to start thinking out of the box, thinking beyond what they've been told, thinking beyond the little bits and pieces that they've been allowed to know. They're going to be able to stop and think, "Hey, maybe this isn't exactly new information. Maybe this is just a little tidbit they're feeding us. Now what more is there?"

And once people begin to ask the questions, their eyes are open, and they start looking further. So it's not that we can give them a pat answer. As a matter of fact, when Mark and I taught mental health back in early 90s on how to help people recover from sexual abuse, from trauma, from PTSD, and all these dissociative disorders, we were telling them that they needed to teach people how to think, not what to think. For example, when people were recovering memories of incest or sexual abuse, they remembered that they had sexual abuse in their past, but because of the kind of compartmentalization that happens, they weren't really sure, and they were trying to remember exactly what happened. Since the mind is so suggestible, if the therapist asks at that time, "Was that Daddy who did that to you?" then it becomes Daddy in their minds. So that's telling them what to think, whereas teaching them how to think is to teach them to question, and say "Who was that? What were the circumstances?" Even details like, "What were you wearing?" Little details like that will bring the truth forward, instead of being told what to think.

And that's what's happening in society, even now, with the

terrorist attacks. As that happens, we're told over and over again what to think, and we need to be told how to think. And how to think is to begin to ask questions, and look further than just what we're told--to be able to learn how our brain actually works, and what the limitations are. It's essential that people shut off their TVs and look into mind control, and arm themselves with that knowledge. Once they have that, they're on the road to freedom.

TRACY: Now, in your memories of your past, do you have screen memories in addition to real memories? How can you tell them apart?

CATHY: The only way to recover memory that's too horrible to comprehend is to make it comprehensible. And the only way to make it comprehensible is to take it from the emotional to the logical. The way to do that is by writing. So I wrote out my memories. And what that does is it switches the information into the logic part of the brain, because it takes the logic part of the brain to move a pen. So the information's becoming logical as it's being written. Once it's logical, it becomes comprehensible. Once it's consciously comprehensible, then a person begins to recover. I functioned under mind control on a subconscious level all those years, and I had no ability to consciously think, or to reason. I had no conscious awareness at all until I recovered the memory. And when I began to recover by using the logic part of my brain, and making the incomprehensible comprehensible, I gained a conscious awareness. With that conscious awareness came the ability to ask questions, and to critically analyze, and to look at things.

It's real easy to separate a screen memory from a real memory under conditions like that. You ask yourself: "What happened before?" "Well, I sat in front of the TV, or a sat in front of a movie, you know, or this equipment was being used." Those kinds of things are really easy to remember, so ultimately, when I deprogrammed, I deprogrammed the program first, and that made it easy to separate the reality from what was being pumped into my head. It's a very deliberate process as a recovery mechanism from the kind of robotic mind control that I had. In the first years that Mark and I were publicly speaking, back in the early 90s, on the issue of mind control, since I was one of the very first to have recovered, we were actually teaching mental health professionals how to help the numerous survivors that they were seeing recover as well. And one of the first steps was to be able to separate the screen memory, to be able to teach them how to think rather than what to think. In those days false memory was proliferating rapidly, because mental health was ignorant and did not know what they were dealing with. The information on mind control had been suppressed from mental health from the earliest years, back when Dr. Ewen Cameron, who's the founder of our A.P.A., was actually working on mind control for the CIA in Montreal, Canada.

Of course, Dr. Cameron and the CIA were found guilty of their involvement in that, and actually had to pay some of their Canadians victims in a lawsuit, which, if you're interested, is in a movie that they released. It's brilliant. It's a documentary that they released in Canada called *The Sleep Room*. It was banned in the United States, but they are aware in Canada of what went on because of Dr. Cameron. And Dr. Cameron is the one who suppressed the information initially from mental health to the point where they had to relearn. They've since even had to rename the dissociative disorder that is a basis for mind control from Multiple Personality Disorder, which is a misnomer, to Dissociative Identity Disorder. This is a much more well-defined term, not only for what the disorder is, but for how to recover from it. Whereas with Multiple Personality Disorder, they get all kinds of demonic possessions, and this and that, and all kinds of superstitions sprinkled in it so heavily that they've had extreme difficulty. I don't know of any cases that have recovered from the superstitious aspect, whereas with what's happening now, people are actually beginning to recover. So I am one of the very, very first, and I am extremely fortunate to have survived, to have been able to recover, and to be able to help bring this information to light.

TRACY: So you didn't have multiple personalities, is that correct?

CATHY: Well, they termed it that at one time, but it's actually a dissociative disorder that creates a compartmentalization of memory in the brain. So I didn't have multiple personalities. I had the essence of who I am, or my personality, that was shattered into so many different parts, so that, for example, the part where my father would sexually abuse me--that part of my mind would compartmentalize around that event so that the rest of my mind could function normally. I couldn't think to bring to mind his sexual abuse until it happened again. And when it happened again, the part of my brain that knew how to deal with it would automatically open. Our brains are really phenomenal. That part of my brain would open to deal with that trauma again and again, and that trauma is all that part of my brain knew. That's not a personality. That's not a whole person there. That's a little tiny fragment of my brain and my own persona that was reserved just for my father, and knew only my father's abuse. It was like going through existence with blinders on. I only knew certain politicians, I only knew certain sexual activities, I only knew to be involved in drug industry. But whatever activities I was forced to carry out, I couldn't think to bring it to mind to discuss it with anybody. I could only do exactly what I was told to do. And that wasn't various personalities, see, that's just simply compartmentalized memory.

TRACY: Yeah, I understand. You didn't walk around thinking that your name was Mary or Helen, or thinking you were a little girl.

CATHY: Exactly, exactly. See what a difference that makes for recovery? If someone's going through the role play of being this person, that person, and all, how are they going to recover? That's not reality. That's the misconception right there. Another really important point is: I was used in a sexual capacity in later years, during the Reagan/Bush administration, because my sexuality had been so heightened from the early sexual abuse. It had actually gone into an area of eating, or drinking, or survival, because of my father's substituting his penis for my mother's nipple. That goes in on the strongest of levels of just basic survival. That's where my sexuality went into a heightened mode, and it just stayed heightened all my life. Whether mind control is used on a sexually abused child or not, their sexuality is heightened.

TRACY: I hope this isn't too personal a question, but I was kind of curious about it myself. You said that there was some kind of carving, some kind of scar that they put on your genital region. What was it?

CATHY: It was a vaginal mutilation carving that was used in pornography. It was used to fulfill some perversions, or whatever. It's something that doesn't go away, and it was something that was done to my vagina where it looks like there is a face that actually comes out. It's hideous, and I remember exactly when it happened, how it happened, and how it was carved. I wasn't given any drugs, or any kind of anesthetic or anything, so I certainly was acutely aware of it, and it was painful. But its appearance has a function, which I don't get (but then again, I don't get a lot of these perversions), and then it also has some physical aspect that can give men pleasure in a little bit different way. So they knew what they were doing, and I'm not the only one that's been carved that way, but I don't know of anyone that's survived who has it. It's definitely evidence that doesn't go away. Kind of like stun gun prod marks, you know, it just is there.

TRACY: So you said that it gives the man pleasure. Is this, like, the same concept as ribbed condoms?

CATHY: Yeah, maybe.

TRACY: Was it distinctive? Would you say that if a person found a pornographic picture of you that was taken, you could match it up?

CATHY: Oh yeah, absolutely. No question about it.

TRACY: You said that Larry Flynt had some pictures of you taken in *Hustler*. Do you know when those were taken, and when they were published?

CATHY: Yeah, different ones in different ways for different purposes. I'm not really sure what all magazines were used, but there were a couple that do stand out more.

TRACY: But you wouldn't know what to tell me if I were to go through some back issues to try to find you in there, or anything?

CATHY: You know, on some of them, yeah. He's got a few that are more underground than *Hustler*.

TRACY: How old is Kelly now?

CATHY: 21 [In 2001].

TRACY: So if she's been locked up in a juvenile institution, shouldn't she be getting out about now?

CATHY: She was turned out when she was 18. She is on her own to a degree, but Kelly still needs rehabilitation desperately for the high-level mind control that she was exposed to. In essence the key that locked the door to her mind needs to be used to unlock it. When I recovered my memory, and remembered the trauma, that actually took down the barriers in my brain, which gave me access to those parts of my brain. Instead of compartmentalization, I now have free-flow full access to all of my mind. In Kelly's case, her compartments were created through harmonic vibration, and they need to be harmonically vibrated back down. So she's still got the compartments in her brain that can be accessed, and she still is definitely accessible. She has an extremely difficult time just getting by, particularly with this administration that's in right now. She's having a really hard time.

TRACY: Wasn't she forbidden while she was in the juvenile facility from using the word "George Bush"?

CATHY: Yes, it's a matter of court record. She and I were both forbidden to say the words "George Bush," "Wizard of Oz," and "mind control." That's pretty weird, in itself, that they would put that in a court record. Kelly's court case--there wasn't anything legal about it. So much so that a District Attorney actually went before the court on Kelly's and my behalf, and told the judge that he was in violation of this law, and this law, and this law. And the judge at that time said, "Laws do not apply in this case for Reasons of National Security."

TRACY: And reasons for that were never given, right?

CATHY: No, but it's rare. Usually those kind of statements are made behind closed doors, rarely as a matter of public record in court. But the fact that the National Security Act has been invoked in my daughter's case is pretty significant in itself. It's pretty validating to the magnitude of what she went through. So the gross injustices that she went through while in the custody of the State of Tennessee are to me just as horrific and horrible as what she endured under mind control. It's awful what that child has been through. Just absolutely horrible.

TRACY: What was she being institutionalized for?

CATHY: This is kind of complex, but brainwashing was one of the first forms of mind control used on an espionage level, and like I said, Kelly had been born and bred for an espionage level from the onset. In the old days they used to give the old cyanide pill, that you may have heard about, which they would take before being tortured, so that they could die with their secrets instead of revealing them. That pill has been replaced with programming. The subconscious mind can be manipulated to the point where it controls the areas of breathing and the respiratory area, and blood flow, so that even military Special Forces, for example, can take a bullet and not bleed. So they figured that they didn't need to have that cyanide pill anymore. Why not just program espionage agents with an automatic circulatory or respiratory failure? In Kelly's case, hers is respiratory failure, activated as soon as she begins to remember her past. When we were in Alaska, after Mark rescued Kelly and me, we felt safe for the first time in our whole lives. We knew love for the first time. It was such a dramatic difference. I really thought I had died and gone to Heaven. I believe that in one of those near-death experiences that I had actually crossed over, and I thought that Kelly and I had died, but of course we hadn't. Since we felt safe, we began to remember, and the memories started flashing, and they were intrusive, and bits and pieces of what had happened started coming forward. Up until that time, I was completely amnesiac about my past. I didn't know where I had been for ten years. I didn't know what had happened. I had absolutely no memory of it whatsoever. When Mark first rescued me, I really thought that I was 24 years old. It was a trip finding out I was 30.

TRACY: They had lied to you about your age?

CATHY: I had no concept of time. Under mind control, since there's no ability to maintain a continuity of thought or a conscious awareness, there's no concept of time. And with no concept of time, there's no ability to know how old you are. And they actually did some studies on aging based on that, because if a person doesn't know how they're supposed to act their age, or how they're supposed to look, they don't, and people don't age properly. Oftentimes people under mind control are age-inappropriate. Their age doesn't show in their face. They can maintain a youthful look way beyond what's normal. So I had no concept of time. I've caught up with that since those days, now that I'm aware. But since we felt safe, we began remembering. When we began remembering, Kelly went into respiratory failure. When she went into that programmed respiratory failure, she was taken to Humana Hospital in Anchorage, Alaska. She wasn't responding to any kind of conventional medication. That's the first time that I heard the term "Multiple Personality Disorder." That's the first time I heard a term applied to what we had experienced. The psychiatrist that was treating her initially diagnosed her with Multiple Personality Disorder, with active mind control programming.

TRACY: That's a diagnosis?

CATHY: That's a diagnosis. And that diagnosis was rejected by the State of Tennessee when she was thrust into their custody. When they took custody of her, they would not accept diagnoses from outside the state, and of course the cover-up ensued from there. But Kelly ended up in the custody of the State of Tennessee because of a Federal program, the Violent Crimes Claims Commission, that was actually overseen out of Washington, D.C. It was a catch net, in essence, and Kelly was scooped up immediately, and thrust into the Tennessee system. Once it was determined in Alaska what she suffered from, that diagnosis was picked up, and the State of Tennessee took custody of her through illegal and immoral means. And she was raised in their custody, then, right up until she was 18 years old, and of legal age, and it left her in quite a mentally devastated condition. But Kelly does know who and what Mark and I are up against. She has had enough memory to be aware of that, which has given her a very deep and profound insight into life, into reality, into what's happening these days. In so many ways she's a wise person, yet at the same time her ongoing need for qualified rehabilitation leaves her unable to hold down a job, for example, or to become a contributing part of society like she would like to be. She's still not free to be what she wants. She doesn't have the ability to have the soul expression to do exactly what she would choose.

TRACY: Is she not accepting help from you and Mark?

CATHY: She and I are very, very close, and we've had a lot of conversations since she's been out of custody and everything. But there's extreme limitations on it because when she sees me, when we're together, when we talk about anything, it triggers memories. Because she feels safe and loved, it automatically starts to flood her mind. When it floods her mind, she goes into respiratory failure. And that's a reality that she and I live with to date, which has got to be one of the most cruel things that any parent and child could ever endure. She knows that, like truth, I'm not going to go away. I'm not going to abandon her needs in any way whatsoever, and Mark and I are totally dedicated to getting the information out on mind control. Instead of operating out of desire for vengeance on the perpetrators, or wanting to expose their political influence and all so much, it's more out of love for humanity, love for Kelly, love for the children that motivates us. Love is the most powerful force in the universe, and it's certainly what drives Mark and I today. Hate, vengeance--those kind of negativities are immobilizing, and they actually hinder progress. There isn't time for that. It's essential to get the information out for Kelly's sake and for everyone's sake.

TRACY: Now, is there significance in the name "Kelly," because I know that Brice Taylor's daughter is named "Kelly," and there are some others also. It's been said that slaves were told to name their daughters "Kelly" for ease in tracking, or something like that. That's what I've heard. What's your answer?

CATHY: I don't know, it's something about--what's it called: "Kiley," the messenger of death, or something? There's some negative aspect to why they wanted it. It's really more occult based.

TRACY: Oh, Kali, the Hindu Goddess of Death!

CATHY: Yeah! And I've got a sister named Kelly. My daughter's named Kelly. I didn't have any choice in that. Yeah, there are a lot of Kellys out there. Just because someone's named that certainly doesn't indicate any kind of conspiracy, or mind control, or anything like that. But nevertheless, there is an inordinate number of Kellys out there that have been used on that level. I think that's even why they used the name "Kelly Bundy" [on *Married ... with Children*], because it was so prevalent.

TRACY: I'm so glad that you gave me that answer, because the other thing about how it makes it easier to track them doesn't make any sense. If you've got 100,000 Kellys that you're supposed to track…

CATHY: That sounds like something that would come more from the Brice Taylor/Sue Ford direction, since you brought up her name. She is someone that I am certainly familiar with. I think that she's done more damage than anybody with her misinformation, based on the fact that the mind control aspect is something that she pulled in initially from false memory through her therapist, and kind of stuck to. I can't imagine what would motivate somebody to do that. Nevertheless, she was sexually abused, that I'm aware of from having known her, and she suffered from Dissociative Identity Disorder, and needed to recover from that. She is one of the most prominently known victims of the False Memory Syndrome that was being perpetrated through the mental health system, and which she continues to perpetrate through the misinformation and disinformation that she's putting out there, which I think is a crime against humanity in itself. I wish she would stop, and I wish that she would ultimately find her own peace and know that truth makes her free. But you know, of course that's not something that I can do. All I can do is just count on the reality that truth always prevails, and love wins.

TRACY: I was wondering what you would say about her, because

I haven't read her whole book [*Thanks for the Memories*], but I did read an excerpt where she says that she went and stayed at your house, or that you stayed at her house, you and Mark, and then she supported you financially for months and months, and went through all this programming. And then she says, "At the end of it all, Mark told me that I wasn't a victim after all." And it sounds so horrible. I was just wondering what you had to say.

CATHY: Actually, I had heard that she had rewritten her original novel, when it was a novel, which I think would have been admirable. She's someone that Mark helped recover from a Dissociative Disorder, because we were working real close with mental health back in those days, and the whole False Memory Syndrome was there. And it is possible for someone to recover from Dissociative Disorder while having had implanted false memories through bad therapy, with the "Was that Daddy that did that?" type of questions. Recovery was possible, and she did recover, but all it did was … I don't know. Somewhere along the way she picked up a weird motive and a weird direction. I can't understand why somebody would do that, but she did nevertheless. So what does that mean about the recovery process for someone like that? I don't know. It just means we've got a whole world of problems out there that we've got to overcome, from the misinformation and disinformation that began back with the Dr. Ewen Cameron mind control at the very onset of the organization of mental health. That's another case where mental health itself needs to think outside of the box, and think beyond the education that they paid to have, and realize that a PhD doesn't mean they know it all.

TRACY: I think one of the side effects of this information about Project MONARCH coming out is that there are a lot of desperate people out there who have been traumatized in their past, but what they really want is attention.

CATHY: It's really hard to understand that, you know? For me it is.

TRACY: I don't find it hard to understand. It's like the same type of people who go around saying that they were abducted by UFOs.

I think that it's the same scenario. I mean, there are just so many people who come out saying that they were victims of mind control, and you can tell that they're just congenital liars. And maybe they did experience some form of mind control, but how do you separate that from the fact that they're liars?

CATHY: Exactly. People are people, whether they've suffered from a dissociative disorder or not. When they recover, people are people, and personally, I don't choose to live in the "victim mentality," or the "survivor mentality." There's too many exciting aspect to life. There's too much to learn, too much to grow with, and this is a phenomenal process. I am so fortunate to have recovered from all of that, and to be free to think for myself and to be myself. Living true to soul and being myself every day is a non-stop, constant pleasure that I never take for granted. It's given me different priorities in life, a different perspective on life. Things that other people think are worth arguing about and fighting about, to me seem really trivial in comparison to the magnitude of what really happens in this world, and the wonder of our brains.

Where we're going to be able to go with this information on mind control is exciting in itself. It will give us a view into the other 90% of our brain that we haven't used. We're always told that we use about 10% of our brain, and with a dissociative disorder, you're blasted into other parts of your brain. So much has been learned, and there are so many exciting things ahead for people to learn, about what their brains are capable of. Once they realize it, they can utilize it. But that's an exciting aspect to the future that keeps me hopeful that people will wake up, arm themselves with the information so that we can get the problems taken care of. The truth makes us free, and once we're free, we're going to be able to expand, and learn and grow in ways that people never dreamed were even possible. The future looks really exciting from my perspective. I can't imagine miring it down by clinging to some negativities of the past.

Access Granted:
An Interview with Mark Phillips

By Tracy R. Twyman

Mark Phillips is Cathy O'Brien's husband, and co-author with her of *The TRANCE Formation of America,* as well as the more recent *ACCESS DENIED For Reasons of National Security.* He claims to have rescued her and her daughter Kelly from the CIA's Project MONARCH and mind-controlled sex slavery. This interview took place in October of 2001.

TRACY: How did you come to know about mind control and Project MONARCH?

MARK: Well, Project MONARCH--that information I'll have to relate a little bit later on. I became acquainted with mind control--certainly not trauma-based mind control, that was something that I was just aware of, but I had absolutely no interface with it whatsoever. I worked in a variety of positions working closely with the intelligence community. The Central Intelligence Agency was one of those communities. The others I can't really go into any detail on because I did sign an oath of secrecy. However, I worked in the capacity as a Defense Department subcontractor, so I'm not bound by the same oaths as would be someone who worked strictly military. I became acquainted with mind control, or external control of the mind through just association with now declassified information that was acquired at the Primate Center in Atlanta, and out in Colorado, and at various other Defense Department subcontracting installations that were researching, and doing what I call "mind mapping." I use that term loosely. I don't think that is a real term. But that's really how I became aware of mind control, and how it was being used, particularly within the Soviet Union. This was during the late 60s and early 70s, when there were large masses of people in certain places within the Soviet Union, primarily within Russia proper, that were being used for a variety of methodologies, including just normal information control. They were more or less sequestered from the rest of the population of the country at the time, and all of the information that they were fed was very controlled, and very contrived.

There were also a number of studies going on in the area of genetics, and I was not privy to any of those specifically. That was how I became acquainted with one of the projects. There were about 120 odd projects that I was aware of, and I recall the names of about a dozen or so of them. But Project MONARCH was one that was used, actually one of the smaller ones. They were not using specifically blond-haired, blue-eyed people--you know the Nazi mentality-type family genetic line. They weren't following that specifically. They were more or less staying within the blond-haired areas, but they were using people of all mixed nationalities. Project MONARCH was one that was used in Michigan, Pennsylvania, small parts of Ohio within a number of religious sects there, as well as in California--in Northern California, particularly. Beyond that, I don't know of any other place where Project MONARCH was an active project. [Editor's note: the use of Monarch programming and its trail of victims is likely more widespread, including Canada.] There has been some information released, but the name of Project MONARCH has never, ever been declassified, and since I did not work in that project, I can talk about it, because it's hearsay. It has never been a term that has shown up in any Freedom of Information Act documents. All the genetic research that I know about, with regards to MK-ULTRA, for instance--none of the Project names have been released, that I know of.

TRACY: And besides blond hair, what other genetic qualities were they looking for?

MARK: They were also looking for certain bone structure. They were looking primarily at the family involved. Even though I wasn't aware that they were specifically targeting multi-generational incest, I knew that they were looking at families. Particularly I was aware of the twin studies, and I was also aware of the research that was specifically targeting persons or families that had at least two generations of very specific artistic capabilities that seemed to be genetically encoded. It was pretty benign stuff, frankly, and it certainly did not prepare me for what I ran into in 1988 when I met Cathy O'Brien.

TRACY: How did you meet Cathy, and what did you think when you first met her?

MARK: Well, the first time I saw her, I believe, was at the airport, when she was meeting her handler and husband by the name of Alex Houston, a so-called "country music MC" and state fair ventriloquist, supposedly an entertainer. I didn't find him very entertaining. But nevertheless, he and I had a business relationship, and I didn't have to tolerate his so-called "entertainment business." I met Cathy very briefly, like "Hello." Virtually no eye contact when she picked Alex up at the airport. It was a most peculiar thing: most business people, when they're in a partnership, usually have dinners, and they have social gatherings with the families of their partners, and this did not happen with myself and Alex Houston. Why, I never really questioned, and since I did not particularly want to socialize with him anyway, it really didn't matter. He and I didn't really seem to share any common interests. He played golf and I didn't, and he was into country music, and I wasn't. It more or less stopped there.

I met Cathy, actually, at a party that I had in my house, to which Alex brought her. That was the first time that I actually met her, or had any chance to talk to her, and talking to her was very much like talking to my hand. She really wasn't very responsive. I was concerned just in the back of my mind because of the amount of white that was at the top of the iris of her eyes. In other words, her eyes were really wide, and she didn't have a proper blink response, which I equated more or less as probably stemming from some sort of trauma in her life. I really wasn't interested in knowing much about her because she did not reflect her ego as having much intellect driving it, and I was not interested in pursuing any intelligent conversation with her. She had a plastic smile, and wasn't dressed like anyone that I associated with, either. She looked very much like a 1950s prostitute, and I did not find that to be conducive with anything that I wanted to have any association with, frankly. I thought perhaps that that was conducive to the country music business, and that was the reason that she was dressed in that kind of attire. I didn't associate it with anything else. I had no reason to. She had very little to say to me.

TRACY: And when did you catch on?

MARK: Actually, I didn't catch on. Mind control is so subtle that when people tell me that "I can see that that person is under mind control," I immediately just walk away from them, because, quite frankly, unless you are very well-versed in this particular science, and you literally test the person ... There are some things you can do to test someone's suggestibility, and this sort of thing, on the spot. And linguistically, you can listen to someone and know if they're this or that. But knowing if someone is under mind control, per se, is virtually impossible unless these people are clinically tested, and that wasn't my forte. I mean, I had an interest in the mind, but certainly not in mind control, per se. It wasn't until I was in China that I was notified, because of my company. I was president of the Uniphayse Corporation, and Uniphayse was a manufacturer of large capacitor bank systems to help the mining industry over there conserve on energy so they wouldn't have to shut down those mines. Shutting a mine down is like shutting a glass or a steel plant down--it costs more to start it back up than it would to have kept it running, and they had a huge energy shortage over there because of when they lived in their proverbial "Bamboo Curtain," and to the West in China it is a constitutional law that they have to maintain a balance in trade.

In other words, it cannot be indebted to any country. In order for them to literally launch into the 20th century, they had to technologically speaking, be able to keep up. They had to be able to provide goods and services, and those goods and services, of course, took energy to produce. And as a result, they had a tremendous need for energy conservation, and that was what my company provided. It was an ancient technology to help them produce more product at a lesser cost. It was the Chinese military, of course, that ran the mining industry, because anything made out of metal, the Chinese military is in charge of. I know this sounds peculiar, but this is Chinese law. Now this is the People's Republic of China. This is not Taiwan we're talking about.

At any rate, my counterparts were Chinese military people, and it was at the ribbon-cutting ceremony of our factory at the Chin-Chin province that I was notified that my partner, who was not present with me at the time, Alex Houston, was involved in both child and adult pornography, which is punishable by death in China. He was also engaged in drug running and money laundering. This would be very much like telling you that there's an alien sleeping under your bed, or something. It totally blew me away. I could not even begin to comprehend it or believe it, because even though I had no personal relationship with Alex Houston, he did not appear to me to be on an intellectual level with the people that I had been associated with by working within the intelligence community. Of course, I worked within the scientific aspect of it, and these people were very, very bright, and most of them very nice people, as far as I knew. I heard stories about people engaged in espionage, the proverbial "Manchurian Candidate" production facilities located on certain military bases, using technologies that were brought over from Project PAPERCLIP. But I personally had no contact with that. I mean, it was just idle chatter with some scientists that I was acquainted with, most of them with NASA.

The intelligence officer who confronted me with the information about Alex Houston, and offered to buy his shares of stock out, which I thought was a takeover, literally, of all of my work to set the company up, and to bring in the engineers from all over the United States to do all of this. I thought my investment of time and money had gone down the drain with their takeover. I had been warned that this could happen. It's called a joint venture agreement, which is what I had. But that was not the case. They literally let me maintain that extra 1%, so I was still installed as President of the company, and I was not going to loose my position, or the company, or my shares of stock. They were even going to fund it, which they did. They gave me the money to buy Alex Houston out, and I did buy him out.

But in the process, when they did all of this, I contacted someone when I got back in the United States from the State Department that I knew through a channel, and told him that I had seen documentation not only on Alex Houston, but also on myself, that was classified. I said, "I don't know whether they falsified it on Alex Houston, or if any of their story is true. I have no way of knowing. But I am going to launch a personal and private investigation on it. But I did want to alert you that the very people that I am in business with are in possession of classified documents on Mark Phillips, and some of that stuff looked like it had original stamps on it, and original signatures." Any time you read a classified document, particularly on the work history of some individual working in the intelligence community, somebody has to sign a piece of paper. Back in those days you would sign it on the border, or on the side, or you stamp it and sign it, and some of those papers they had were originals, or at least they certainly appeared to be.

Moving on, I was totally just blown away by the fact that a couple of days later, or some time past, I don't know, a day or two, I got a call back from an unidentified person with the State Department who related enough detail to me for me to know that it was, indeed coming from that office, to leave the case alone, never mention it again, that it had no significance, and don't probe it, in essence. I'm paraphrasing. I've got them written down here somewhere. But nevertheless, I was completely shocked into the reality by what I had heard from that Chinese intelligence officer, and by my partner in China, who was a major arms dealer for the Chinese, and he owned a ship line. His name was Mr. William Yoon, a very good man, by the way, in spite of his profession, and he informed me that they had no reason to lie about it, and that he knew for a fact that it was true. I trusted Mr. Yoon implicitly. I had no reason not to. He had never misled me and never lied to me. He was very clever and very wealthy and successful businessman, Korean by birth, and lived in Hong Kong at that time.

It was Mr. Yoon who told me that it would be nice if someone could help that woman out, and that little girl that she had, but it would be impossible since, in essence, he was just echoing what that Chinese intelligence officer had told me, that Alex Houston was connected all the way to the White House. Well that was absurd to me. At the time, it just was totally off-the-wall. However, when I got back home, and had that fly up in my face, I did launch an investigation through some friends of mine who were still active within the intelligence community, both within the military, and with the CIA. I was then informed that this was in fact true, and that I had best leave it alone. At that point in time, I was trying to make a decision as to what to do, because I needed to go back to

Hong Kong for business reasons, and I could not be laden down with a couple of people that were literally traumatized out of their minds. I certainly wasn't qualified to help them myself.

So through a string of events that are outlined in our book, *The TRANCE Formation of America*, I moved on to making a personal decision, actually based on one pivotal point: the local sheriff came and told me about the surveillance that I had been enduring. I lived in a rural area. He informed me that my life was in jeopardy, that friends within the FBI had informed him, out of the Nashville office that I was as good as dead if I did not leave that woman and that girl alone, and stay away from it. That was the inspiration to move forward, and I do not take threats lightly, nor do I ever discuss them with anybody. Cathy and I have a rule: we do not discuss any harassment or threats, period, because I don't want anybody getting credit for it. I'll go after them my own way.

 And as a direct consequence, since I knew what I was up against, I thought I'd just try to outsmart them, and get Cathy and Kelly into some form of qualified help. I certainly had the money to do it, and I thought I had the connections. But unfortunately, there was so little known about helping people, and the physicians around the United States and Canada that were doing public research developing a treatment modality for what they call "polyfragmented"--it was called Multiple Personality Disorder back in those days, which couldn't be further from the truth. I'm glad they changed the name. But nevertheless, I couldn't find anybody. The first person that did contact me was Dr. Jolyn West out of UCLA. And of course he's dead now. Hopefully I'll have his records soon. They normally release them a couple of years after they're dead, under the FOIA. But I was contacted by Dr. West's office because I had put an inquiry out, and apparently one of my inquiries hit the wrong button, and I wound up getting the bad guys all over me.

TRACY: You mean you were threatened?

MARK: Um, how many times? The bottom line is, I came from that world. It was absurd to threaten me, because for one thing, threats are meaningless. These people don't threaten you, they just do it. I told Cathy at the time, "Actually these people are being very polite. These threats are a polite way of saying 'Please, please don't go any further with this.'" So I took what I had and turned it over to some people, like the Head of U.S. Customs at that time. I turned it over to him through channels that he trusted. In other words, I did it through political channels out of Washington, and through intelligence channels out of Langely as well, to ensure that the information got into the hands of the people that could be acquainted with some of the players involved in this stuff. And since I had very little hard proof at the time, I proceeded just to focus on getting Kelly some help, and in the process was handed information, piece by piece, on how to help Cathy. Because Cathy had not been structured by anybody, as far as a doctor making the usual mistakes of asking "How does that make you feel?" and doing re-associations with the traumas that she had endured, she recovered quite nicely.

It took about a year, actually about 9 months almost to the date from the time that I started. And I got this information through a series of 800 numbers that were given to me in a most clandestine, covert way. I don't even know who I was talking to, and I didn't know if the information was real. I mean, it sounded logical, and it was easy to apply, but I didn't know if I was hurting her, or if I was helping her. I had no clue, except that she seemed to be getting better, and by that I mean that she stopped her constant state of dissociation. She acquired a sense of time. She acquired a sense of self, and who she was, and where she'd been. Then I started collecting those details up, handing them over to people that were in a capacity, working for the government, to get them verified. And when they started getting them verified, one or two of them made their usual mistakes, They tapped on the wrong doors, apparently, and that created some very serious problems. As a result I was almost indicted for something that I didn't do. That's usually what they do.

TRACY: What was it?

MARK: Well, they said that I had written a threatening letter to the President of the United States. That was untrue. I had written a letter to the President of the United States, even though I knew that he was named and involved in the thing, but I had a federal lawyer eyeball the letter, and then I had a United States congressman read it, and then hand-deliver it to the President. I think it was that simple. So I was clear 100%. So when the FBI took me down and fingerprinted me, I actually thought it was probably one of the funniest things, a pathetic type of humor. Because, I mean, my fingerprints, they must have had 10,000 copies of them. To put me through that intimidation process was ridiculous. I had lost everything that I had, and, you know, if you back somebody up against a wall after you've taken everything away from them, and then you threaten them, then they have nothing to lose. A man that has nothing to lose is extremely dangerous, if he knows the rules, and I did know the rules.

TRACY: What were you doing to deprogram Cathy?

MARK: Well, the process of actually deprogramming somebody--you don't ask them any questions. It's not like most people would think. I had to know certain codes, keys and triggers. I *had* to, and I was provided a few of those, enough to get the information flow going inside of her own head. She had to write. She wasn't allowed to verbalize. I wasn't able to ask her any questions. Really, what it amounted to was, I was no more than a bodyguard and a nurse, and a housekeeper, and a cook, if you want to get right down to the nuts and bolts of it. The process is outlined in our book. We'd be on this phone for quite a while if I went through each step, but basically I had to just sequester Cathy away from all forms of information. In other words, her suggestibility was so high that if she saw an ad on TV for Kentucky Fried Chicken, she could taste it and smell it in the house. I mean, it was the Pavlovian Dog thing. So I had to keep her away from all sources of information. She had to pretty much live inside of her head during this period of time, and I was, of course, just trying to keep us alive through what little savings that I had left. I was just making sure that the bad guys didn't know that I was interested in any of the content of what she was saying.

Quite frankly, the stuff she was telling me was outside of my realm of experience. I had never knowingly been acquainted with anyone who had been a victim of family incest. I wasn't raised that way, nor would I have been able to recognize it, even. So the stuff that she was telling me sounded 100% totally preposterous. The only thing I did was, I made sure that there were certain things that could verify whether or not her memories were correct. For one thing, she would write them down, and three weeks later, if she could remember exactly what she wrote down, word for word, verbatim, and the beginning and the end of the particular event that she was describing, and the smell and the tastes involved, in other words, the olfactory sense, if it was involved, then I knew it wasn't what is called a "screen memory," or a false memory. Everybody has false memories. Everybody has screen memories, and two people, if they see an accident, will recall it differently, for instance. But when someone is under trauma, they have a photographic memory, and if they are at the point of that trauma, the photographic memory also is compartmentalized cellularly. In addition to that, they also have complete memory as far as the olfactory sense goes, and that's pretty much the tell-taler right there. One of the oddest things that I ran across with Cathy was, she had forgotten that she had ever been able to dream in her entire life.

Many years later, Cathy and I got onto the lecture circuit, and of course we attracted mental health and law enforcement first, because I thought that would be the safest way of getting this information out, and the most credible way of getting it out. I never dreamed of going public with it. Quite frankly, they shoot messengers, and this kind of stuff would be hard for most people to accept, because they have these impressions that entertainers and people involved in high-level politics might be sociopaths, but they're not pedophiles. Or, they might be this, but they're not that. So I didn't think it would be a good idea to go public with this. I think I'm jumping around a bit. I was mentioning the dream state thing being the oddest part. When we got on the road, a number of people would come and tell me that they knew they were under mind control because they dreamed this, and they dreamed that, and they dreamed this, and I'm thinking: "Yes, you definitely have a problem, but I'm not qualified to diagnose you. How about taking this test?" And this test is commonly called a D.E.S. test. It's a test for your level of suggestibility, and dissociativeness that all of us have.

TRACY: What do the letters stand for?

MARK: I was afraid you would ask that. Oh my goodness. I can almost see it myself. I do not have the luxury of a photographic memory. But nevertheless, the DES test was developed around 1990--1991, and it was a result of some information I had released, as well as a number of physicians who were studying the rise in the phenomena of what was then called Multiple Personality Disorder. Particularly they were studying individuals coming out of the military. These people were projecting different personas, but they were unaware of each other. But in fact it was one personality that was fragmented, and what they were seeing were the coping skills that each persona or fragment had developed. They were naming them, and labeling them, and all this incredible nonsense. It became almost humorous, except that it was so sad for the patients. These doctors would stand up and say, "Well, I've got a patient with 712 personalities," and another one would say, "That's nothing. I've got one with 1215 personalities." And it became a spitting match, and it was almost absolutely absurd. Cathy probably had thousands of persona fragments, and many of them were because of the change in histamine. Her face would change, and her eye color would change, and her skin would change. There were a lot of changes that the religious community for many years called demonic possession. I mean, it is quite frightening. If you see it for the first time and you don't know what you're looking at, it's terrifying, as a matter of fact. I won't say "quite frightening," it's just plum terrifying.

However, there is a very logical, scientifically-based reason for this change, and there's also a reason why the person doesn't dream at night, or have any recall in dreams. I happen to believe-- and this is a theory of mine that has yet to be proven, publicly--I happen to believe that everyone dreams, regardless of whether they're under mind control or not. But under mind control, they have absolutely no recall whatsoever of any dreams. Now, if someone is suffering from horrific abuse, yes, they'll dream at night. If they've endured a severe trauma where perhaps they endured a near-death experience, they will have horrific dreams as a result of it. And people who suffer from Post-Traumatic Stress Disorder have horrific dreams. All the stuff that's been happening as a result of the recent terrorist attacks has caused untold numbers of people to suffer from varying levels of Posttraumatic Stress Disorder, with horrific nightmares that either could be or could not be directly associated with what they saw on television.

TRACY: If dreams are supposed to happen mostly during the Rapid Eye Movement stage of sleep, and if these mind controlled slaves can't blink when they're awake, maybe that can't do it when they're asleep, either.

MARK: Well, that's a very good observation. What you just said is very true. Most dreams occur during the R.E.M. state. The R.E.M. state occurs after about 2 or more hours of rest. It normally occurs between two and four hours, and you normally have around 17 minutes per episode of R.E.M. state. And this particular sleep state is not possible for someone under mind control to have, because if they do allow these people to go into R.E.M. state, then the sleep deprivation thing is over. Their brain chemistry will return back to a normal level, and these people will rebel and run. You know, the fight or flight syndrome kicks in. So, yes, when someone is under mind control, the R.E.M. state is interrupted, and it is interrupted first through a ritualistic program. Whoever their handler is has to interrupt their sleep through some kind of trauma, so that they are not allowed to go into R.E.M. sleep. And once this pattern is established, it becomes part of their nightly routine. With Cathy, and Kelly as well, that was the first thing that I noticed. They did not sleep soundly. They would just sleep restlessly for an hour or an hour and a half, under the 2-hour minimum that it requires to have R.E.M. sleep, for your brain chemistry to change.

TRACY: I was curious about whether or not you had any experience with personally: I'm always hearing about these Project MONARCH slaves, and how they have levels of programming that correspond to Greek letters. Did you have any experience with that?

MARK: No. As a matter of fact, these stories circulate, and we hear them, and at one point in Cathy's relationship with me, when we were spending most of our days in court, I mean, literally, for a couple of years, I didn't have much else to do except research this stuff. And so, yeah, I followed the trail of some of these stories, and they always dropped back into the same mental institution, and the same person. It was a doctor who was recognized as credible who had released this information, without any validation whatsoever. Actually, someone who's been a victim of mind control would not know it. They would never have any conscious awareness of it, unless they had gone through the deprogramming process, or unless they had some sort of brain surgery. There are a number of extraordinary conditions that might trigger some memories, but people who claim mind control, with the Alpha-Beta-Delta-Theta programming denote some stuff that does have some basis of reality to it.

As far as the symbols going for the victims themselves, of course they wouldn't know that stuff. But there has been reference, very credible reference that cannot be proven because that kind of information has been redacted from the FOIA files for MK-ULTRA. I can tell you categorically, "Yes, there's Delta programming, yes, there's Beta programming. Yes." But no, I'm not going to say that victims of this stuff were aware of any particular Greek alphabet.

Where's Johnny?
An Interview with Noreen Gosch

By Tracy R. Twyman

Noreen Gosch is the author of *Why Johnny Can't Come Home* and founder of the Johnny Gosch Foundation, which can be found at johnnygosch.com. Her son Johnny Gosch was kidnapped in 1982. The case was very high-profile and was featured several times on *America's Most Wanted*. However, media interviews became harder to obtain when Ms. Gosch began voicing her opinions about the alleged connection between her son's kidnapping and Project MONARCH. This interview took place on September 3, 2001.

TRACY: Why do you think your son was chosen to be kidnapped?

NOREEN: From the reports that we have gotten, from Paul Bonacci, who was one of the victims, and a witness providing us with information, Johnny was chosen because he fit the description of what they were looking for in the pornography and prostitution industry. Paul Bonacci testified to this fact in a courtroom February 7th of 1999 before Federal Judge Urbom.

TRACY: Do you know what the specific traits were that they were looking for?

NOREEN: Well, he was blond, blue-eyed, and tall. They looked for kids that were from the type of homes where they would be, basically, in a normal situation. Not a one-parent home, but the typical two-parent home, you know with the pet dog and that type of thing. A paper boy. They had been, according to Paul Bonacci, kidnapping kids that had been runaways, kids that were fairly streetwise, and they decided--by they, I mean the people that were involved in this particular kidnapping--they decided to go for kids that might not be as streetwise, perhaps just a little more naive. This is what Paul Bonacci said when the Judge asked him that question, and it sounds pretty logical when you consider the kidnapper's point of view. I suppose they feel that those kids are easier to intimidate and/or manage when they have them under their control.

TRACY: I read the sample chapter from your book posted on your web page. You seem to believe that the police department was purposely bungling the investigation.

NOREEN: Oh, it's not that I seem to believe it. It happened. The morning of the kidnapping, we had five witnesses, and every one of them saw the man, talked to the man, saw the man flicking the dome light on and off three times. A second man came out from between two houses and followed Johnny around the corner. Then the witnesses heard the slamming of the car, the screeching of the tires and this car pulling away from the scene heading North on 42nd Street [in Des Moines, Iowa], which takes you right out to the interstate. One of the witnesses was a 44-year-old attorney who is now a judge, and yet when all of this information was presented to the police, the police chief said they considered him a runaway, and they weren't going to do anything for three days. My contention is, when there's a bank robbery, they don't call it runaway money for three days.

When Johnny was taken, we had what most families don't have, which is that we had five witnesses on the street, and each of them witnessed a different part of the kidnapping. One of the witnesses happened to be a 44-year-old attorney who is now a judge. Pretty reputable. Pretty credible. And yet, they wouldn't look. They wouldn't call in the FBI. They refused. They wouldn't do aerial searches. They wouldn't use free volunteer canine teams to begin to search for our boy. We as a family had to do this all on our own. And something is wrong in an investigation when this happens. Many years later, I learned that our police chief, the one who is no longer in office, Cooney, is extremely good friends with the Police Chief from Omaha, Robert Wadman. And Robert Wadman was involved in the Franklin Credit Union cover-up, which was a porn and prostitution ring operated in Omaha, Nebraska, that was uncovered in the late 80s. And our Police Chief went over to the parties that they had. The Police Chief from Omaha got one of the girls pregnant.

TRACY: So he himself was a pedophile and involved with the same group that kidnapped your son?

NOREEN: That's right. And I learned all of this later, much, much later, and then two and two made four. It became pretty simple why the Police Chief wouldn't call in the FBI, why he wouldn't do certain things. They didn't want me to find Johnny. They didn't want me to uncover what had really happened to him.

TRACY: And you learned all of this from Bonacci?

NOREEN: Bonacci, and then there have been a number of other witnesses, victims that we have talked to since Bonacci came forward, and they all tell the same story, with the same people involved. And these other witnesses are credible. Paul Bonacci was real credible in a court of law.

TRACY: And what about the *Des Moines Register*? Two of their paper boys were kidnapped, and they didn't seem to have much interest in the subject.

NOREEN: Yes, isn't that curious too?

TRACY: Well, why do you think that is? Do you have any theories?

NOREEN: From what I know about pedophile rings, people who are very influential can be involved, in any city, stretching all the way to Washington, D.C., as we found out. It's very possible that there are people right here in Des Moines that are involved. Someone else is protecting them.

TRACY: You don't think that they might have set your son up to be kidnapped in the first place?

NOREEN: I have not ruled that out. That's still under consideration. You can consider it, and you can get pieces of information and evidence, but when it becomes difficult is when you try to prove it in court. You can know it, but if you can't prove it by all the means necessary, then you have to just sit on your information. We know, basically, what happened to Johnny, why, who, how, and much of it was brought out in that court case in 1999. Once we got the Judge's ruling, I went back to the county attorney, the police officials here, and asked them to talk to Paul Bonacci. That's something they have never done. They have never interviewed the boy. And today [September 3, 2001] there was a big article here in the *Des Moines Register* about a retiring police detective. That police detective happened to be the one that worked on the Eugene Martin case [another, possibly related kidnapping.] And it said in this article that he would probably go to his grave not knowing what happened to these two boys. Well, part of the reason why they'll go to their grave not knowing is because they didn't investigate one of the key people who could have answered all of their questions. They refused to talk to Paul Bonacci. We have tried for many years to get them to sit down with him, so that he can tell them what happened.

TRACY: Is he still there in town? Is he available?

NOREEN: Paul Bonacci lives in Omaha, Nebraska, which is about two hours away. He would talk to them if they asked, but you see they don't, and the reason they don't is because they simply don't want the story of Eugene Martin and Johnny Gosch to come out. They do not want any implications towards anyone that they're trying to protect. That's sad to say, but that is the situation that I'm up against here. And my only hope and help is to be able to go public with everything that I know, and to remain in a public situation where I speak out about it, rather than cowering in silence. There's safety in bringing out the truth. Are you familiar with John DeCamp at all, and the Franklin Credit Union? He's a good fellow. He's worked in this almost as long as I have. It will be 19 years Wednesday since Johnny was kidnapped, and John De Camp came in to this in the 1980s, when Paul Bonacci, who was accused of another crime wrote a letter to him, and asked John DeCamp to come represent him. John agreed to represent him. And it was during one of their initial visits that Paul Bonacci told him that he had been in the car, and helped to kidnap Johnny.

TRACY: Did Bonacci mention anything about this pornography ring being linked to the CIA and Project MONARCH?

NOREEN: Yes, he did. He also told us that he was put into MONARCH training at a very young age, right at Offutt Air Force Base. Offutt is one of the training centers. I have also over the years received communication from some of the former Air Force men who worked at Offutt, and they confirmed what Paul Bonacci told me. Since I've gone public I get lots of information just by people contacting me, and these two gentlemen had worked at the Offutt Air Force complex during the 80s. They said that is where they brought kids to put them through the rigorous MK-ULTRA training.

TRACY: So, do you believe that's what happened to your son as well?

NOREEN: Yes, that is the information we have, through Paul, through private investigators, and many years of searching, and interviewing other victims who were also with Johnny at many periods of time. They all reveal that he was put through the same training.

TRACY: Didn't your son come back and visit you at some point in 1997?

NOREEN: In 1997, I had been on a network TV show just a couple of months before this had happened--the Lisa Gibbons program. She asked me if I wanted to give a special message to Johnny on the show, and so I did. I said to him that I just knew that he was alive, and that I would help him no matter what had transpired in his life. I gave my address on national television where he could find me. And within three months, there was a knock on my door at 2:30 in the morning. I about had a heart attack--seriously, I did. I could hardly believe my ears when I heard him say "It's me." I asked through the door who was there, and this voice said, "It's me. It's Johnny. It's me, Mom." And I looked out the peephole on the door, and our hallways are very well-lit at this apartment complex. I could see him out there, and his eyes had not changed. Yes, he was older, yes. He was grown-up and physically developed into a young man, but the eyes had not changed, and I knew it was my son. He did have a young man with him, and he did not volunteer his name, he did not want me to know who it was. They both came in, and we talked for about two hours. And I offered to have someone come who I felt I could trust, because I thought Johnny was home to stay. And when I said that I would call somebody, he became very alarmed. He said, "You don't understand. No one can know I was here. I'm bringing you information that I want you to take to law enforcement. Hopefully they will make some arrests. But no one can know it came from me just yet."

And so I promised him I wouldn't tell anybody, and I didn't. For two years, I told no one. My own mother didn't know. And it wasn't until I was in that court room in 1999, and John DeCamp asked me the question, if I had seen or talked to Johnny in all of that time, and I had to answer, because the judge made me answer the question. There was a reporter in the room, so of course she wrote everything down. And I did take the information that I received from my son to the County Attorney. I asked for a special meeting. I just could not tell him that the informant who came forward was my son. I had to tell him that it was just someone else, because I did honor my son's request. And the police typically said they weren't sure what they would do with the information, if anything, which is always their response. And so I told them that I had my own attorney with me, because I felt that was what I needed for my own protection. I did inform the County Attorney that I had come in voluntarily, and shared my information with them, and so therefore they could never accuse me of withholding info. And I told them that they could conduct their investigation in any way they chose, and I would continue doing the same with mine.

TRACY: Did your son tell you all about the mind control?

NOREEN: Yes, he did. He told me that he had been subjected to mind control, and many of the horrendous things that he had been forced to do. He did, however, hold back on some of the information, I think probably out of embarrassment, you know, for himself, and some sensitivity for me. Because some of it would be pretty graphic, as you can probably understand.

TRACY: Did you understand that he had been sold as a prostitute to high-ranking businessmen and politicians?

NOREEN: That's correct. That's what he told me--that he had been used in that manner, and that his job was to compromise politicians, and any VIP that they felt they wanted to do that to.

TRACY: And were there Satanic rituals involved?

NOREEN: He only mentioned the Satanic rituals briefly. He didn't go into depth about them as far as the details of what they did, but he did say that was part of what they did, and that was also confirmed at an earlier date by Paul Bonacci, and the other victims that I have talked to. Because there have been others that have come forward besides Paul, but they did not want their name in the press. But they had also been part of this ring, and they had also been with Johnny on many occasions. And to date, we have interviewed 45 of them. We have quite a few, yeah. As you see, all of this information was presented to the police. All of this was given to them. And they still say that they do not want to talk to Paul Bonacci. They're just not interested.

TRACY: So the attitude of the police hasn't improved at all over the years?

NOREEN: No, it hasn't. They're content to leave this as an unsolvable case, and it's just the opposite. It's quite solvable, if they were willing to investigate Paul, and take the information that he has given, which is part of court transcripts where the judge ruled that he was telling the truth. If they would take that information and work, then they would have it. But they are not interested in doing that. I've even gone to the governor of our state, and the governor's response was, "Well, this is really none of my concern, two missing boys in Iowa." And then he suggested that I take my problem to the Department of Public Safety. Well, they do traffic lights. They do zoning for traffic situations. They help make those decisions for the city. So they won't help either. And yet for the Governor [Tom Vilsack], it is within his power. He could direct the department of criminal investigation to work on this. He has that power. But he has chosen not to. Now why do you suppose that is? I'll tell you why. We found out that this Governor is extremely close friends with the former governor of Nebraska [Bob Kerry], who was involved with this whole Franklin mess. They have been long-time friends. Our Governor brought Governor Kerry's sister over here and gave her a top key position here for six figures, and there was quite a collusion there.

TRACY: I've heard from a lot of proclaimed Project MONARCH victims that Presidents of the United States have been involved.

NOREEN: Yes, that's what I have heard as well. I've gotten a lot of help and a lot of information from John DeCamp, and another man is Ted Gunderson, who is a former FBI agent. He's one of the good guys, however. In the early 1980s he retired, and went into private practice as a private investigator, but he still has the connections to get information. So with his help, coming on board with Johnny's case, and John DeCamp with his knowledge of the Franklin situation, we were really fortunate, and we started putting the pieces of the puzzle together concerning Johnny. And we found out that Johnny's case is right smack in the middle of this whole Franklin situation. Law enforcement doesn't want to touch it. They don't want to touch it in Omaha, Nebraska, and they don't want to touch it in Iowa. They'd just as soon let this rest, and wish that I would just go away and forget about it. But you see, there were two young boys that were ripped off the street here in Des Moines, Iowa. My son first, and then within two years, Eugene Martin. Both boys are gone. Identical circumstances. We know that the cases are connected. And yet we have a governor who says that this is none of his concern. Don't you think that's a very odd statement by a politician who might want to get re-elected some day? Why is it not his concern? Why? Well, let's go back to his association with Nebraska. What is he possibly involved in that hasn't come out? I don't know. It's either one of three things: he's either incredibly stupid, incredibly naive, or he's involved in something, and he's hiding it to protect himself and/or his friends. I would choose the latter. Because you know he's not a stupid man, and he's not a naive man.

TRACY: It must make you very uncomfortable to know so many people in positions of power are involved in this somehow.

NOREEN: Oh, it does. It's very disheartening when you realize that you've worked all these years, and you have the truth, and they choose not to accept it. When I went to the County Attorney, I was shocked. 'Cause I took the transcripts from the court, and the judge said that Paul Bonacci was telling the truth. And he just looked at me and said, "Noreen, we just aren't going to accept the judge's ruling." It took the wind out of me. I couldn't believe it. I said: "Wait a minute, this is a Federal court ruling, doesn't it apply in every state?" And he said, "Well, we're just not going to accept it." So then I appealed to the governor, and he told me the same thing, that this was none of his concern, and I should go to the Department of Public Safety. So, does this sound like passing the buck, shuffling the hot potato? It doesn't take a rocket scientist to figure out what's going on here in Des Moines, Iowa. I don't have any qualms about saying this. I've said it on TV programs, I've said it in various articles where I've been interviewed, and I'm very cautious about my safety. But the public needs to know that this is going on, because it's not only going on in Iowa, but no doubt other states, and if they could do this to me, and to my son, they can do it to anybody. The men who took my son, and Eugene Martin, and many other kids, have not been caught, have not been punished, and there is absolutely nothing to prevent them from striking here again, or in any city they choose.

TRACY: Did either Paul Bonacci or your son tell you that Michael Aquino was involved in this somehow?

NOREEN: That information first came from Paul Bonacci, who told us that Aquino--he kept referring to him as "The Colonel"-- came to the location in Sioux City, Iowa, where they had held Johnny captive for about 14 days. That's where they took the first pictures of him while he was being molested. And Paul Bonacci stated that he came there and gave the kidnappers cash for having done the job of kidnapping Johnny. He basically bought Johnny from them. And then he took Johnny with him to Colorado. The next time Paul Bonacci saw him was about a year later, at this Colorado location that he said belonged to the Colonel. Then we also heard the same information from probably 25 of the 45 other victims that we have talked to and interviewed.

TRACY: Do you know where this location was in Colorado?

NOREEN: It was a couple. They had one that was called a safe house, and it was kind of an old house up in the mountains of Colorado. *America's Most Wanted* did a show on Johnny, and then they did five updates. And on one of those last updates, *America's Most Wanted,* with Paul Bonacci, went to this location, and they filmed it, and it was on television. And they showed that in the basement they had cages where the kids were locked up when the adults would have to leave. That was just one of the houses. They had them in New Mexico and Arizona. They called them "safe houses." But there was also living quarters there in Colorado. Kind of a ranch, they called it, where Aquino supposedly had his place, and they went to this place quite often, where they would have, you know, different activities planned. And the kids would be flown by plane to these locations for parties. They were also transported at night. They would drug the kids, and they would then sleep. They would just have them all in the back of the van, and they would travel to wherever they were going. They would travel by night, and then have the kids to the location the next day for one of their parties.

TRACY: I think I remember reading that there was a relative of Anton LaVey involved. I remember reading it. They said it was his son, "Michael LaVey."

NOREEN: Anton's son agreed to be filmed and interviewed by *20/20.* They were involved in much of the information gathering with their detectives. And during the interview with them LaVey said that he had been with Johnny on many occasions at the Satanic ritual ceremonies, where they serviced different men for their owners. And the only reason he agreed to speak in front of cameras was because the father is now dead. Then I found out very recently that Anton LaVey's daughter lived in Des Moines. She was here during the 90s. And Anton LaVey came to Des Moines and stayed here for quite some time prior to his death, which I did not know until about four months ago [May 2001].

TRACY: I'm really confused, because to my knowledge, Anton LaVey doesn't have any sons by that name. Is this an illegitimate child or something?

NOREEN: I don't know what the circumstances are, but there are two daughters and a son that I know of. I know of one man through a third party who dated one of his daughters. Since I've gone public with this aspect of the story, people hear about it, and they are very willing to contact me with the facts. That's how I found out that his daughter had lived here. And then I did some checking on it with my detectives, and sure enough, he was here.

TRACY: Well, I'm really curious about this Michael LaVey character, because one of my good friends was friends with Anton LaVey for years, and he's the one who told me that Anton LaVey doesn't have a son named Michael. So I'm really interested in tracking this guy down, because either he's lying about being Anton LaVey son, or Anton LaVey's has a son that nobody knows about.

NOREEN: It's very possible that he does have a son that nobody knows about, or that is not publicized. The information that I got on that was given to me by *20/20* after they had done the interview. And they had victims, 45 of them, all on tape talking about this whole thing, including MK-ULTRA, including all the sex, and prostitution, and pornography, and the Satanic rituals, which many of these kids participated in.

TRACY: And I presume that none of this footage got aired.

NOREEN: It hasn't yet. They have a one-hour special called "The Johnny Gosch Show" ready to go, and I don't know when they're going to release it. I know that there have been other people who have tried to get the rights to it, and *20/20* won't release it to anybody. They're holding onto it. They want to wait until Johnny is located, and then they want to run it. They don't want to jeopardize his life any further. And within all that material is the LaVey interview.

TRACY: From your impression, what do you think the role of Satanism is in this? Do they really religiously believe in the Satan concept, or is this just kind of a fetish?

NOREEN: I think it's more a means of control of kids. That's what I think it is. Because, you know, you grab a kid from somebody, some little 12-year-old kid, and you take him away from his mom, his dad, everything he knows, his toys, his room, and you start to brainwash him. To start to break him down. You can tell him anything, at that point, and have him believe it, so that you can gain complete control of him. So that you could walk into a public place and know that he wouldn't run, because of what you've indoctrinated into him. All these young victims that have been kidnapped, like Johnny, they've been gone for over half their lives. They've been away from their families. This is all they've known. Their education stopped at 12. They have not been educated in any school. And the one thing that I learned from these victims, because I asked this question of just about all of them that I've talked to: When you got sick, or when you needed a dentist, what did they do? Did they take you to a dentist, to a doctor?" And the answer was the same with every kid. "Oh no. They wouldn't risk taking us to a doctor's office. They brought their doctors to us. They had their own." Further proving that pedophiles come in all sizes, shapes, and career levels. The medical profession is not exempt. But they had their own, and they brought them in, because, you know, think about it: kids are going to get sick. They're going to need medical care, they're going to need things. And this is the answer we got from every single one of them.

TRACY: So what is it that binds all of these people together. Just an interest in pedophilia?

NOREEN: No. Money. Kiddy porn is a multi-billion dollar industry in this country. How did it get that way? Supply and demand. There are pedophiles that are rich enough that they don't have to dirty their hands and go out and grab a kid, or solicit a kid. All they have to do is call somebody who supplies it to them, brings the kid to them. The internet is a new playground for pedophiles too.

TRACY: So you can order a kid online?

NOREEN: They have chat rooms. They go into chat rooms, and they begin to make an approach with children, begin to lure them into conversation. The reason I know this is 'cause I work with an internet detective. He poses as a 13-year-old child in a chat room. He has pedophiles approach him. He learns the name of the pedophile, and in some cases, the pedophiles have even Federal Expressed airline tickets for him to travel to their home. As soon as he gets an identification, he contacts the National Center for Missing Children in Washington. They then contact the police and/or FBI in the town, and the arrest is made. They've brought down some pretty big ones in the last year. They got one of the top executives with Burlington Industries, and they got one of the top executives of Eastman Kodak.

TRACY: Burlington. Are those the people that make the coats?

NOREEN: Textiles. Mmm Hmm. Both cases were due to go to court in May [2001], and both executive plea bargained, probably pushed enough money around in the court, and they did not have to go through the court process. But that's two biggies in this country, and they were caught by the internet. There's another one that involved a pretty famous surgeon in the Midwest. This is a doctor that you or I might go to and put our lives in his hands. He was arrested for luring a 13-year-old girl to a motel room for prostitution.

TRACY: So if money is the motivating factor, why is the CIA involved? Are they involved in the child pornography industry just to raise funds for their various projects?

NOREEN: That, and they were heavily into the mind control aspect of it. That's how it all got started in the first place. The mind control, remote viewing, all of that was being used and taught to our spies for the purpose of protecting America. And then there were people within that organization that thought, "Oh, this would be cool. Let's use it on kids."

TRACY: So what they get out of it is the chance to experiment on children?

NOREEN: A lot of experimentation has gone on with kids, yes, as well as soldiers, and prisoners in our prisons. They've all been exploited over time. And the way this all got started, I'm sure that you're aware of the German scientists and how this whole mind control project developed in our country, or why we even have it.

TRACY: So when you met with your son for those few hours, did you see in his personality any evidence of this? Did it seem like he had multiple personalities?

NOREEN: Yes.

TRACY: Really?

NOREEN: I would say that he probably does. I didn't see too much of it displayed that night, but knowing how they work, knowing all that the other victims have told me, I do believe that it would have been difficult for him to have escaped it. Now, the only reason why Johnny is free now is because he and several other boys did escape in the late '80s. They stole a car in the city, and that's how they got away. They went to one of the boys' homes, Jimmy. He had been a runaway, and he was later grabbed by these guys. He got to know Johnny, as well as some of these other kids. When Jimmy took these kids to his father's home, he just told him that they were buddies of his that had needed a little help, a place to stay for a couple of nights. So his father let them stay there, gave them some meals, and then some of these kids, one of which was my son, moved on. Jimmy's parents didn't look too hard for him when he turned up missing, because he had run away in the past, and they just figured he'd turn up sooner or later. I've talked to this man many times. He's a CPA, a very well-respected man. He did not realize that the boy that was staying in his home was my son. He didn't realize it until he saw his picture on America's Most Wanted, which was just a couple of months later. At that point he called me, and he felt so terribly bad, because he said, "I had your son right here. I could have called you, but I didn't know it was your boy until I saw the show." And the man was quite reputable. Johnny did stay there. He was there. And I know the circumstances of his escape. That's probably the only reason why he's still alive. After these kids outlive their usefulness, are no longer marketable for prostitution and pornography, then there's only a couple of choices: they either make a break for it, or they're killed, or they're turned into perpetrators, and made a criminal.

So in Johnny's case, he and these other kids had the guts to try and get away. This is what some of these other victims have told me, that Johnny had tried repeatedly to get away, even shortly after he was captured, and that he took a lot of beatings because he kept trying to get away, to get back home. So this wasn't anything new, him fighting back, and trying to be free of them. If you're familiar at all with what happened to Paul Bonacci, when he came forward, people said that he was nuts. People said that he was not credible, wasn't telling the truth, that he was a dingbat. Multiple Personality Syndrome obviously meant he was nuts. John DeCamp and I worked eleven years before we got the judge's ruling. Eleven years it took to get the ruling. Well, now, Johnny knows Paul Bonacci, so do all these other kids who have escaped. Johnny and these other kids are too afraid to come forward, seeing what was done to Paul for telling the truth. They saw him being charged with another crime, and having to spend five years in prison for just keeping quiet. I believe that these other boys and my son will come forward. I'm quite sure of that. It's because of the fear of the way that the system will treat them. Because they haven't done anything wrong. They were kidnapped. They were forced into this. And yet, they're afraid that they won't be believed.

TRACY: So what do you think it would take to bring your son back, to get him to come forward?

NOREEN: What it would take would be some high-profile publicity showing that the police actually took a hold of the information that was provided by Paul Bonacci, and are working it like they should have back in 1989 when Paul Bonacci first came forward. You see, we've spent over a decade here [now nearly two decades] that's been wasted.

TRACY: I suppose that if the police did finally decide to investigate this, and they chose a couple of individuals to prosecute, then Johnny could come forward, and he would receive immunity.

NOREEN: He would receive immunity, and also protection. Because that was his other big fear when he was here. He said I didn't understand why he couldn't just stay here. You know, "It's over. You're back home. We'll go to a county attorney in the morning, we'll talk it over, blah blah blah." He said, "Mom, you don't understand. There are so many of the high officials in this country that are involved in this. I know because I've been with them. They're involved in this. What makes you think my life would be safe if I was in their hands? They would kill me for what I know." He said, "Your life is not safe either, for all that you're doing, and coming out publicly. You have to be very, very careful." And that was the other reason he did not want me to tell anyone that he had been here, for as long as I could possibly keep it. And I will have to tell you, when my mother found out that Johnny had been here, that I hadn't told her, she was absolutely shocked that I could keep it silent, and tell no one, absolutely no one. When I had to live with that for two years, and try to figure out a way to help my son without jeopardizing him, it was very hard for me, because I didn't know who I could turn to, or if I could turn to anyone and trust them. My attorney did not know Johnny had been here. When we went into that meeting, he believed, just like the county attorney was told, that there was an informant that had come forward with this information. Because when I went into that meeting, I turned over a list of names of people that were involved, what their part was, how they kidnapped Johnny, how they selected him, where they took him, the house where they had him, who came and bought him, every bit of it was given to the county attorney. And all I told him was that an informant had come forward. I was not at liberty to tell him that it was my son, because it would have jeopardized Johnny's life, and he was my first priority.

TRACY: Can you name some of the names that were on that list, besides people that we've already mentioned?

NOREEN: I can't, at this time, because these people have not been charged with a crime. The county attorney has them. The police have them. But if I name them publicly, then they can come after me with slander and/or any kind of libel suit.

TRACY: But these are nationally-known figures, some of them.

NOREEN: Some of them are, yes. Some are local.

TRACY: Did you come across any information indicating that some of the revenue being derived from this child prostitution was being funneled to the Nicaraguan Contras?

NOREEN: We did come across some of that information. That was provided to me by Karen Burns, at ABC's *20/20*. You see, when *20/20* stepped into this, and asked for exclusive rights to do a one-hour special on Johnny's story, they had someone investigate, so that we could get the information that we needed, close the case, and then I could go to the county attorney and say, "This is what we've learned." Well, when I did that, we know what resulted. They said they wouldn't accept it, or the judge's ruling.

TRACY: Do you think *20/20* would be willing to talk about this show that's in the can right now?

NOREEN: No. There have been others that have tried to get information out of them, and they say, "Oh no. There's no story there." And there are a number of reasons why they don't want to talk about it. I have one young man who told me that he tried to get the story. He's also with ABC, but just another show, and they wanted to do the Johnny Gosch special. So they went to *20/20*, and they were told: "Back off the Gosch story. It's classified. No one else can have it, and *20/20* owns it." He represents a different show on ABC, and he was quite upset that he couldn't get it.

TRACY: Yeah, I'm surprised that they wouldn't even talk about it.

NOREEN: They're not ready to do their thing yet, and so they're not going to give a clue to anybody else.

TRACY: Oh, if they talk about it then some other show will do it, and that's what they don't want.

NOREEN: Yes. Then they'll be scooped. And that's why they're keeping a tight lid on it.

TRACY: But if they aired the show, it might blow this whole thing wide open, and that might make the atmosphere safe for Johnny to come back.

NOREEN: That's exactly right. I have a feeling that there's been perhaps some involvement by the CIA or the FBI here too. When *America's Most Wanted* was preparing to do Johnny's story, just days before the show was to air, the FBI called *America's Most Wanted*, called John Walsh, as a matter of fact, and told them to kill the Gosch story. And Paul Sparrow, who was the producer at that time, called me and said that he had talked to John Walsh, and they decided they were going to do the show regardless, even though the FBI was threatening them. But the FBI did not want the information that I was going to give to go nationwide. They wanted to kill the story. That came first-hand from John Walsh and the producer. That's another red flag: why would the FBI want to cancel the Gosch story? Why would they find it so threatening--the information that Paul had to share? You have to ask these questions, because it makes people start to think, "Wow, what if it would have been my kid, or my nephew, or my niece that had been taken, and the parent did all that Noreen has done, and this is what they do?" I am not a person who has ever been a conspiracy theorist. I was not even into reading about them. I know there are plenty of books out there, but I had not even delved into anything like this. When Johnny was kidnapped, it happened in such a swift manner, from the time that he left the house, that I knew the kidnappers were organized. I knew there were two of them, from the witnesses.

What I didn't know (and it took many years, and the help of John DeCamp and Ted Gunderson, and some detectives from 20/20, and my own detectives) was that it was tied to this level of prostitution and pornography. I knew when they took my son, they weren't going to take him to Disneyland to show him a good time. I knew that it had something to do with sexual abuse of children, of course. But I had no idea that it was that sophisticated in our country, let alone the fact that they used mind control on the kids. I mean, this isn't something that you just pick up any paper and find out about. In fact, back in the '80s, no one even said the word "pedophile." I knew there had been sexual abuse of children, beause I saw it in the news, but no one used the word "pedophile." I didn't even know what it meant. I had no clue what the word meant until my son was taken.

Then I got another eye-opener when I went to Washington D.C. in 1984, and I was called in to testify before the organized crime hearings. At that hearing, the FBI presented physical evidence as well as testimony. They had a table full of paraphernalia that had been confiscated from pedophiles. On the table were books on how to molest toddlers and leave no marks, how to lure a child to a car. These were all bound books. Somebody went to the trouble of publishing them. And then there were sexual torture toys--that type of thing. But the book that startled me the most was a small book, it was kind of like a spiral bound thing, and in it there were lots of pictures of kids. But these were kids that had not been kidnapped yet. It was like a catalogue. And everyone there at the senate hearing, the press, everybody was shocked. And yet, after the presentation of this, our congress did nothing. It was like the senate hearing was just an exercise for the day. "Well, OK, let's get all these parents, and let's do something to make everybody feel good, make them think we're going do something." But they never did. Johnny was photographed before he was kidnapped. Johnny was photographed on his way home from school.

TRACY: And wasn't one of the people involved in the kidnapping posing as a policeman before it happened, and talking to your son?

NOREEN: Yes, at a football game.

TRACY: Do you know who that was, then?

NOREEN: It was a West Des Moines policeman.

TRACY: So it *was* a policeman?

NOREEN: It was a policeman, and he paid particular attention to Johnny.

TRACY: So there were other members of the police department involved from the very beginning.

NOREEN: I'm sure that there were, yes. And this particular officer would not consent to being interviewed by our detective.

TRACY: Since you've delved into conspiracy literature and the subject of Project MONARCH, do you buy into any of the theories involving the Illuminati--that this is some secret occult brotherhood that goes back thousands of years? Do you entertain those thoughts at all?

NOREEN: I think there's a distinct possibility that some of the people involved in this could very well involve themselves in that. But there's probably also a lot of them that work these kiddy porn situations that are not, that simply do it for the money, or the trade-off in drugs, or whatever else they're getting in exchange for the use of children. So I think you might have a mixed bag there. I've done a lot of reading on the Illuminati. I don't discount it. I believe that it exists, and that they intend to bring the New World Order, but I just don't believe that all pedophiles necessarily fall under that umbrella. I think we have too many that are creative and find ways to use kids as innovatively as they can.

TRACY: Did you come across any information that in addition to kidnapping children, they raise them, they breed them for this purpose?

NOREEN: Yes, we came across information that there were breeder mothers whom they have impregnated for the designed purpose of bearing children to be kept within this organization. Therefore there are no birth records that they can trace, like they can with somebody missing. They make sure that there is nothing recorded. Many of these are babies that are sacrificed within their Satanic rituals. And I've heard this from a lot of the victims. In the back of my book, I invite victims of this horrible thing to contact me, and I give my email address, and I answer all emails. I was just deluged. I was getting 50 emails a day. And many of those came from victims who are now adults that have been through the multi-generational abuse, that weren't kidnapped like Johnny was, but nevertheless as children, this was the way they had to live. And they bear the scars, emotionally, because of all that they were put through.

TRACY: Have any of your informants come up with a name for this organization, or is it just a number of different ones?

NOREEN: It's a number of different ones that operate throughout the country. This particular one that was involved in taking Johnny was based out of Omaha, Nebraska. That's just one. But there's more. They ship the kids around. It's an international situation. And yet you'll have politicians, you'll have the FBI stand up in front of a microphone and say crime is going down these days, that crime against children is on the down-sweep. Well, that just isn't true.

TRACY: Are they not counting these?

NOREEN: They're not counting them, right. They're not recording them properly. Because when a child is taken, and moved from one place to another, that constitutes abduction, that constitutes kidnapping. When a child has been molested, and many times, murdered, the charge that is given to the man that is caught, if they catch him, is Murder One. The fact that the child was kidnapped first and sexually abused beforehand are minor charges that come down later. So they're not always caught in the record-keeping of kidnapping. And those types of crimes are cases where it is maybe a pedophile who is acting alone. He's not operating within a big organization. I call him your garden variety. The ones that live in Our Town, USA all their lives. And they might be the guy that volunteers for the scouting, or whatever, just so that they can get close to kids. And they molest over, and over, and over, and they get the kids to keep quiet. And then you have the ones that kill. And finally you have the ones that belong to these organizations.

I've had to go to five different prisons since Johnny was taken, to meet with inmates, to get information. The one that I will never forget, that still raises the hair on the back of my neck happened to be a serial killer. He had molested little kids, girls, and he had also killed them. But he had information, so I went to see him. During our conversation he gave me all the information he thought he could, and I said to him: "I have to know why you killed those children. Because you wore a ski mask, so they didn't know who you were. They couldn't identify you. So why kill them?" And he got this smile on his face, and he said: "You don't understand. At the moment my victims know that I'm going to kill them, that look of fear in their eyes, that is my turn-on." Well, I never forgot the look on that guy's face. He's not much above an animal in the way that he would hunt down a child like it was his prey. But the look of fear in the eyes of a child, when they know they are going to die, that is his turn-on. It made me sick. All I wanted to do was go out and take a shower after being in that room with him. But see, how many of those do we have running around the country? I don't know what the estimated number of serial killers is, or if they even know.

TRACY: So do you think this is what happens to most kids that disappear?

NOREEN: I think it happens to a great number of kids that disappear, and nobody looks. They write it off as a runaway, or a case that can't be solved. Most of the guys that were on Johnny's case from the beginning have either retired, or they have died now. So we've got a new, younger crop of men that are at the department. They have young kids. They are raising families. They know that they don't want their kids hurt. So they are a little more sympathetic to me. I have one detective in particular. He has twin sons, and he has been very good. He has tried to talk to the police chief. The new police chief, by the way, is from Omaha, Nebraska, and a good friend of the old police chief from Omaha. He begged his chief to start a task force within the department to do nothing but work on Johnny's case and Martin's case until they were solved. He was told by the police chief to stop trying to help Noreen solve this case. In other words, "Back off." And the detective said, "Why?" and he said "We don't want this to go any further." Well, he came to me to tell me that. He said that: "If you ever bring it out publicly with my name, I'll have to deny it to protect myself." But he said, "You need to know what you're up against. They're not going to help you. They're not going to do one thing with the information that you have worked so hard to get, and that you've proven to a court of law in Nebraska. They're just simply not going to do it, because they don't want this case to go any further." That came directly from the police detective. He came to me with this after I had published the book, otherwise it would have been in the book, just without using his name.

TRACY: It must make you feel kind of hopeless.

NOREEN: Well, it doesn't make me feel that it's going to end any time soon, but I keep hoping. I have a great deal of faith. I'm very strong. And I just can't believe that there's a supreme being in the universe, a god, that would let you go through all this, and let you work this hard to try and find the answers to help your child, and along the way do the work that I've done to help other kids--I just don't believe that this could be allowed without finally being given a resolution of some kind. I already have the knowledge of what happened to him. The resolution is what's beyond my grasp right now.

TRACY: Do you believe he's safe now?

NOREEN: All I know is that he's hiding, and that's what he has to do to remain safe right now. So I know he's probably not living the kind of life that I would want for him, you know, like in a nice home, with education, and maybe a nice wife with kids. Because he's almost 30 [now 38]. He's probably living hand-to-mouth, with very little money, just trying to get by. Nobody wants that for their kids. It kind of hurts me to know that I've got one son out there that has the bare minimum of what most people would consider adequate living. Now that I know that he's away from them, I know that he's not being mistreated anymore, so that's a comfort. But he can't come home for dinner. He can't come home for Christmas. He's too afraid to even come near the family. He's afraid they'll grab him. What all the victims have told me is that after they kidnap the kid, after they've given them the initial drugs, and their first sexual abuse contact, they take them out and they force them to commit a felony. And therefore they have leverage. They tell the kids, "You try to get away, and we'll turn you in. If you try to get away, you can never go to a police person to help you, because you've committed a felony. You're wanted." And you tell a twelve-year-old kid that, they're going to believe you. If that's all you've been told, from the time you were ripped away from your parents, you would live in that fear. You would not go to a policeman for help.

The Franklin Cover-Up:
An Interview with John DeCamp

By Tracy R. Twyman

John DeCamp is the author of *The Franklin Cover-Up*, and a former Nebraska State Senator. He has been a good friend to Noreen Gosch and a colleague to Ted Gunderson. This interview took place over the phone on October 3, 2001.

TRACY: Would you first tell me briefly how you came to investigate "the Franklin Cover-Up"?

JOHN: Purely accident. I was hearing some of the stories on the street from some of the senators, and I was one of the first ones to stand up and say, "This is absolute nonsense, and this couldn't be, and if I really believed any of this, I'd be the first to do something about it." So I got a call then from a kid who was in jail named Paul Bonacci, who asked me to at least come see him and talk to him. I went to see him, talked to him, talked to a psychiatrist sent by the state to examine him, 'cause they thought he was acting strange. He was a multiple personality. I became convinced that I should look further, and kept looking, and once I got involved, I just kept getting deeper and deeper. I ended up representing a number of the children involved. So I started out on the opposite side completely.

TRACY: Did you come to the conclusion that what was happening to these kids in Nebraska, where they were getting kidnapped and being used as prostitutes, was an outgrowth of Project MONARCH?

JOHN: I came to the conclusion that for sure some of the children who were truly involved in this--and for every real one, there's somebody who makes up their own story or something--but anyway, for every kid legitimately involved, there always seemed to be a linkage or a relationship to some sexual improprieties, and compromise, that being a key ingredient of MONARCH. Of course, [former CIA Director William] Colby, who was kind of my best friend and mentor, assured me that there was no such thing as MONARCH officially; that's the name the kids knew the program by, but that was not the official name, and you won't find anything in the official record by that name.

What he did say, however, was, after the Korean War, the American CIA and the American government, in fact, were very terrified. We [the CIA] believed that the ability of other countries, particularly China, Russia, North Korea, at "brainwashing," as it was known at the time, and mind control was developed to such a degree, that, he said, "I know this sounds silly, and you'll laugh when I tell you, but we at the Company (meaning the CIA) actually believed that the Russians had developed techniques so that they could put someone in the same room with, let's say, the President of the United States, and through E.S.P. actually know what he's thinking. And you can imagine how dangerous that was, and we decided we couldn't afford to be behind. For the very salvation of the country we had to catch up. And so millions and billions were poured into these programs," and he said, "I'm sure there were some horrible abuses, but that wasn't the intent." The intent was to "save the country." And then he said one other thing. He made particular mention of one fact. He said, "I'll tell you one thing, John. When all is said and done, we were never behind, and we aren't today."

TRACY: What role do you think Satanism played in "the Franklin Cover-Up" and Project MONARCH? Some people seem to be of the opinion that it was just used as a mind-control technique to traumatize the children.

JOHN: I think that's probably a fair statement. I don't know. I don't claim to know enough about any of this. I don't know if there's a Satan, but I know that there are cults that claim to be Satanists, and they do some pretty bizarre things. I'm always one of those who's the opposite of the conspiracy theorists. I look for practical explanations for virtually everything.

TRACY: So you don't think that all these people were part of a particular group or cabal of occultists?

JOHN: Not particularly. I find that difficult to believe, but I'll admit that I don't know. All I know is that there are some horrible things that are happening to some young people. It did happen, and I'm sure it's still going on: the combination of mind control, using techniques from some of the "Satanism-type activities," or whatever. One of the key things involved creating multiple personalities. As I understand it, you can create a personality that's literally like a robot, that does what you want, or can be programmed for particular activities, and I am quite certain from talking to enough people, and seeing enough information that such techniques exist. What banner they run under, whether it be Satanism in some occasions, or mind control, or military intelligence, or National Security, or whatever, I think it boils down to the same thing. The most malleable mind of all is that of a young person, particularly someone about 11-15 years old. You get the right material, or tool, or equipment, and you apply the right techniques, which seem to almost inevitably involve things that we would normally consider sexual aberrations, and then you throw in some other techniques learned over the ages, and particularly the practice of skills by some of the better psychiatrists, or psychologists, or whatever, involving some drug use, and pretty soon you have a mixture of a product that you can breed horrible creatures with--people who will do what you want and accomplish certain goals.

TRACY: Do you think that this is what happens to most of the children that go missing? That they're inducted into these pornography rings.

JOHN: I don't know. Certainly some are. Whether that's what happens to most or whatever I don't know.

TRACY: Don't you think it's strange that so many public officials and wealthy businessmen are involved in this type of activity, like child prostitution, and particularly that they seem to be interested in homosexual activity with male children? That just seems so out of proportion to the rest of society.

JOHN: I think it's a fair statement what you just said. There seems to be an inordinate percentage of individuals that adhere to a little different sexual code who are involved in these particular practices. Whether they got into them, and then got compromised into staying in them, I don't know. But when you just start looking you certainly start seeing a disproportionate percentage. But then, you're talking about some pretty strange practices too.

TRACY: Yeah, I just was wondering why people in positions of power seem to be predisposed to this.

JOHN: I don't really know. I just know that if you were doing a study, that's one of the things that you would first take note of. There seems to be an inordinate percentage of that particular cast of characters, when you'd think normally that it should be quite the opposite. It should be the dregs of society that you'd find involved in this, and instead, so typically the most shocking surprise is when you discover that the personalities involved are often the best and brightest and most respected, and most trusted.

TRACY: So in your position now I imagine you still deal with a lot of people who are in politics or who are wealthy businessmen. Does this make you wary of them.

JOHN: Oh, not more than anybody else, no.

TRACY: Do you think that some of the money for these activities was used for secret government operations, or Contra Aid, things of that nature?

JOHN: I believe that it's fairly well known. I don't think there's any contest among those that know that the CIA, and to a degree the FBI, determined for a significant period of time that they were vested with the responsibility to save the country, and that the politicians were kind of incompetent, and they needed a funding source where they wouldn't have to be accountable. That was the key thing. They needed a funding source where they didn't have to be accountable to Congress in explaining what they were doing, and that resulted in things such as arms dealing and drug dealing, whether being on the fringes of it, or making sure that it could occur, and then getting a pay-off. I have no doubt in my mind today, painful as it is for me to say it, that the CIA engaged in this conduct.

But the problem started when they decided that they had to save the country because the politicians were too dumb, and they couldn't get the necessary funds to do what they thought they had to do. Of course, any time you go off on that track, then you have the abuses crop in, and what was a noble goal turns into a whole bunch of stealing and theft, and that sort of thing. And that's what I believe occurred. It was the old "end justifies the means" thing that got out of control, the end being that "we have to protect the country from the bad people, and we're the secret agency vested with the responsibility, but we don't have enough funds, because politicians aren't smart enough to know that we have to do these things, and so we have to have a funding source where we don't have to explain anything." Well, what's the funding source? The most quick, easy, available funding source to get that kind of money without having to explain anything is drugs.

TRACY: And prostitution.

JOHN: Oh yes.

The Finders:
An Interview with Ted Gunderson

By Tracy R. Twyman

Ted Gunderson is the author of *How to Locate Anyone Anywhere Without Leaving Home*. He is a former FBI Special Agent, radio talk show host, and expert on Satanic conspiracies. This interview took place on August 25, 2001.

TRACY: I know you worked for the FBI. How did you first get introduced to the subject of Project MONARCH?

TED: Right after I retired, I opened a private investigative firm in Westwood, Los Angeles, California, which is by the UCLA campus, and my first major investigation was the Geoffrey MacDonald case. He's a former Green Beret doctor who was convicted of murdering his wife and two children at Fort Bragg. The murders occurred on February 17th, 1970. Anyway, I got involved in that investigation, and I had 19 witnesses. It's probably the most highly publicized legal trial case in the history of the United States other than maybe O.J. Simpson's. Within 10 months, as a matter of fact, on October 25, 1990, I obtained a signed confession from the girl who said that it was her Satanic cult group that was involved in the murders. He did not commit the crime.

Now once you get involved in such a case, the first thing you're going to do is look at the evidence, look at the testimony, see where evidence was lost, stolen, destroyed, and altered by the government. The Satanic cult group that was involved in the murders was also involved in a large-scale drug operation, bringing drugs in military planes, including C.I.A., from Southeast Asia into the various bases in this country during the Vietnam War. And the cult that wiped out the family went in without the permission of the higher-ups in their operation, which included police officers, two attorneys in Fayetteville, North Carolina, and high-level military personnel. The cult did not obtain permission from them to do that. They went in randomly and did this. And the higher-ups in the military were afraid that if there was an investigation of the cult it would expose the whole drug operation. By the way, there's documentation in *Time Magazine*, January 1, 1973 about the drug operation. Anyway, the girl gave me the confession. By the way, she died January 1983 under mysterious circumstances.

TRACY: How'd she die?

TED: She was in her apartment, and she died of slight pneumonia, weak lungs, and cirrhosis of the liver. She had called us about two weeks earlier and said that she was under surveillance by two guys in suits in the neighborhood. She was nude from the waist down, and the kitchen faucet was running. That's a Satanic sign, by the way.

TRACY: Why's that? What does it mean?

TED: The signs that they are involved with are Earth, Wind, Fire, Water, and then a combination of all of those. Those are just part of their ritual, you know. Anyway, her six-month-old child was on the floor, dehydrated, but alive, and did survive. I don't know what happened to the kid, but she died that way. So anyway, I went public with the information, and I was on a number of major TV talk shows. I was on CNN debating Freddy Casaba. I was on a number of other shows, like *Geraldo*, and also on radio talk shows. I came forward with this information that Dr. MacDonald did not commit these murders. They were committed by a Satanic cult group. So as a result of that, people just virtually came out of the woodwork from all over the country. People who didn't know each other from the East Coast, West Coast, South, North, and so forth, and told me about the Satanic cult groups in this country. A lot of them were victims themselves--adult survivors, we call them. So that was my introduction into what was going on, and I'm saying to myself, "If somebody from New Hampshire is furnishing me with the same information as somebody from California, and they don't know each other, I mean, there's got to be something to this.

So then from there, I was involved in other cases, including a case from Nebraska. It's called *The Franklin Cover-Up*. That case involved military training at Offutt Air Force Base. I ended up talking to some of the kids who were victims themselves, talking about the MK-ULTRA mind control program. They received their training at the base. They opened up to me. They told me all about their training. I have documentation of it. It's in a book called *The Franklin Cover-Up* by John DeCamp, a former State Senator in Nebraska. So anyway, in that case, it not only involves MK-ULTRA, but it involves a large-scale kidnapping ring. One of the kids that's been talking to us and giving us a lot of information is Paul Bonacci. One of the victims was a twelve-year-old newspaper boy named Johnny Gosch, who was kidnapped on his paper route in Des Moines, Iowa. It involves some of the leading people, and businessmen, and so forth, in Omaha, Nebraska., such as the publisher of the *Omaha World-Herald*. His name is Harold Anderson. It involves the Society Editor of the *Omaha World-Herald*. They were identified by the kids. It involves a fellow name Eugene Mahoney who was the head of the Forestry Service, who was on the Vice Squad of the Omaha Police Department. And these kids identified these people as involved in not only their training at Offutt Air Force Base, but also in the Satanic movement. This large-scale kidnapping ring was kidnapping kids all over the country. They were being held in safe houses after they were kidnapped. Some of them were auctioned off in Toronto, Canada, some of them were auctioned off here in Las Vega, Nevada. I've talked to, and have in my hip pocket, Rusty Nelson, who was the lead photographer for the group. He's been identified as involved, of course, and he has thousands of photographs of sexual exploitation and sexual involvement by some of America's leading politicians.

TRACY: Like who?

TED: George Bush, Sr.

TRACY: So you've seen these pictures of George Bush sexually abusing children?

TED: Yeah. Well, he's got them involved in sexual exploitation. I haven't seen the pictures yet because they're in a cave in Colorado. Rusty Nelson's in Oregon, and if we ever get enough money, we'll go over there and pull these pictures out.

TRACY: Do you know where this stuff is located?

TED: No, Rusty is the only one that knows. It's at about 12,000 feet. So the only time you can go in there is the spring or the summer. You can't go in there in the winter. But anyway, he's got the pictures. We are talking about a large-scale pedophile ring, and a large-scale kidnapping ring. The ring, by the way, is known as "The Finders." It's a CIA covert operation running out of Washington, D.C. I have a copy of a U.S. Treasury report on an investigation of the Finders that was quashed and closed down. The FBI refused to investigate it.

TRACY: Why are they called "The Finders"?

TED: Because that's just a cover name for finding children, and actually what they're doing is picking them up and kidnapping them. It's part of the Satanic cult movement in this country today. The Satanic cult movement dovetails with U.S. intelligence to some degree. It's like any other organization: there's good and bad in every organization of people. They, in addition to being involved in this kidnapping ring, were taking kids out of Boy's Town, and out of foster homes and orphanages, and flying them out of Sioux City, Iowa to Washington, D.C. for sex orgy parties with congressmen and senators. Massachusetts Senator Barney Frank has been identified by the kids, and George Bush Senior has been at the parties while he was Vice-President. He became more discreet as time went on, I guess. That's my introduction to it--a combination of those two cases, and going public with the information, and these people just coming from everywhere.

TRACY: You're saying that there are large elements of the CIA, and the government in general that are part of a Satanic cult. Is it just a number of Satanic cults, or is there one large organization?

TED: No, that's hard to define and clarify. First of all, you have to go back. When I learned about this, I started saying to myself, "Well, why, how, when, what, and where?" So as a result of my research I learned about an organization called the Illuminati. And I've got all sorts of information about the Illuminati. The Illuminati was an organization founded in 1776 in Germany, and its purpose was to take over the world. A fellow named Adam Weishaupt set forth 24 goals at the request of the Rothschild family out of

England. And the goals were to control the mainstream media, to corrupt the youth through sex and drugs, to put their own people as agents behind the scenes, to put them in as leaders, etc. Anyway, that's what it's all about. And their activities dovetail with the Satanic movement, into the U.S. intelligence community, the CIA in particular. I think that the deterioration of the FBI over the last 25 years or so is the reason. I think it's the Illuminati. I think the FBI's been used as a political pawn. When I got on in 1979 we were not involved in politics whatsoever. We used to tell the Attorney General to go jump in a lake when he would call up and tell us to do something ridiculous.

TRACY: So, did you not know about any of this when you were working for the FBI?

TED: Not a thing. It was only after I got out and started operating on my own that I learned what was going on.

TRACY: Did you then reflect on some of your experiences in the FBI and realize that there might have been some connections?

TED: No, I didn't, because when I was in the FBI, I never ran across this. I think that's what's happened since then. In my day the FBI was a straight organization. We didn't have any problems like they're having now. We didn't have any Wacos. We didn't have any Oklahoma Cities--which is a cover-up, by the way. McVeigh was a political pawn, just like Lee Harvey Oswald. We didn't have any Ruby Ridges. We did have the Kennedy Assassination. I did learn, since I got out, by the way, that that was a joint CIA-Chicago mob hit. Of course, I have all kinds of information about the CIA involved in drugs. I mean, you know, Iran-Contra is an example of it. All this information just kind of melds in and dovetails, and one element is scratching the back of the other element.

TRACY: So would you say that the CIA has been under the control of the Satanic Illuminati since the very beginning?

TED: No, not from the beginning. Like with the FBI, I think it's happened in the last 25 years. I think they've been infiltrated by this Illuminati movement, and again that dovetails with the Satanic movement, and you're talking about human sacrifices. I'll give you an example. Here about a month ago [September 2001], in a two-day period we had about 14 children disappear here in Las Vegas. It was on the news, then it was on one time on ABC, and then nobody ever heard any more about it. So when I heard about it, I called the Metro police here. First of all, I called my informant, who was the official photographer in Nebraska for the group back there. By the way, he's been arrested, and he's on bail, and he's on probation right now for pornography. I called him, and he told me about the landing strip that's out in Las Vegas where they were flying these kids out of. So I called the Metro police here in Las Vegas, and I told them: "Look, I have information that they were flying kids out of here, 10 or 12 years ago, at least, but it's certainly worth looking into today, and if you want to send somebody over to the house, I'll be happy to sit down with them and give you all the information on it. It's a landing strip in between here and Pahrump, Nevada. Pahrump is about 50-60 miles away, out in the country some place.

TRACY: Yeah, Art Bell is out of Pahrump.

TED: By the way, he sued me. Oh yeah, I'm the guy. Remember when he went off the air? He blamed me for all of that. But it was a BS lawsuit. He claimed that I made statements about him being a child molester, and I never did. But anyway, that's another story. Anyway, I called Metro, and said I have this information, and well, I haven't heard from them yet. Doesn't it kind of make you wonder about what's going on? Why wouldn't they look into that right away, when you've got missing kids, you know?

TRACY: I don't know, but it seems like they don't take the whole missing kid thing seriously in the first place.

TED: That's because too many people are involved. *Reader's Digest* in July, 1982 had an article about 100,000 children who disappear every year and are never heard from again. Well, I mean, that's serious. And we're not talking about runaway teenagers.

We're talking about 2-to-7-year-old kids. And they've covered it up.

TRACY: So you think most kids that are kidnapped are being taken by the Satanists?

TED: Oh, there's absolutely an international child-kidnapping ring. These kids are auctioned off on the auction block for $50,000 each. Anywhere from actually $15,000-$50,000, according to Rusty Nelson.

TRACY: And where's all this money going? What's it being used for?

TED: It's going into the pockets of these individuals, you know, the Illuminati members, and others.

TRACY: Are all these kids, you think, being mind-controlled as well?

TED: Yeah, that's part of the program. In Des Moines, Iowa we got the Johnny Gosch case, the newspaper boy. His mother, Noreen has been involved in this research. John DeCamp has been involved in this research. We're talking about reputable people. I'm a reputable individual. Nobody listens to us, but we're out there shouting from the rooftops.

TRACY: Did you talk about Project MONARCH and the government and stuff when you went on the *Geraldo* show?

TED: No, I talked about Satanic cults. I was on four of his shows, and I was on a show with Michael Aquino. He's been accused. In fact, Johnny Gosch told his mother that Aquino was one of the kidnappers, that Michael Aquino was the one that bought him.

TRACY: And Noreen Gosch also says that there's someone named Michael LaVey who told her this, Anton's son. But Anton LaVey doesn't have a son by that name, officially.

TED: Anton LaVey does have a son. He's been castrated.

TRACY: Excuse me?

TED: Yeah. Anton LaVey has a son called Anton LaVey, Jr. And you know he died a couple of years ago. I got the documentation. I've got 216,000 pages of documentation on MK-ULTRA. I receive probably four or five phone calls a week from these people, because they're all looking for help. I mean, they're desperate people.

TRACY: Now, do you believe all these people, or do you think there are some people that are just trying to get attention?

TED: Half and half. Some I believe, some I don't, some I think are plants. I've had a number of people planted on me.

TRACY: So there is a lot of harassment.

TED: Harassment? Oh my God, are you kidding me? It's unbelievable. I go to get in my car, and the direction signal's turned on in the morning. They used to run surveillance on me until I started chasing them out of the neighborhood. I'd put my gun on them and go after them. That happened twice, and I got them cornered one time, and I reached under the seat for my gun, and there was too much traffic. Maybe I would've shot them, maybe I wouldn't. Who knows. But anyway, they realized "This guy's crazy. We'd better stay away from him." So now what they do is these little tactics like come into my hotel room when I travel and leave little signs. And I've been burglarized here in my house. They took some of my research. "They" are probably joint CIA-covert operations. These people are highly-trained and professional burglars and assassins, or killers. I knew the head of George Bush, Sr.'s assassination squad. He had 3000 men around the world he could call on to do their dirty deeds.

TRACY: The President had an assassination squad?

TED: Oh yeah, they all do. The current Bush President [George W. Bush] probably has one, I'm sure. Clinton had one too. They operate out of the White House. It's the National Security Council. The NSC doesn't answer to anybody but the President.

TRACY: With President Clinton and all of the women that he was involved with, do you think a lot of those were mind-controlled sex slaves?

TED: Not only Clinton, but I think past Presidents. Brice Taylor says that she's had sex with every one of them except Jimmy Carter since she was 15 or 16 years old.

TRACY: Aren't there a lot of people in the entertainment industry involved as well?

TED: There are some. I don't know if there are a lot. But I worked the McMartin case. I'm the guy that went in there in 1990 in the spring and hired an archaeologist, and we found the tunnels under the school. The kids said there were tunnels under the school.

TRACY: What exactly did they look like?

TED: Well, they were tunnels that had been filled in. We were there for 34 days with the whole team of archaeologists.

TRACY: Was this covered by the news at all at the time?

TED: Yeah, but the mainstream media wasn't going to touch it. Nobody would do anything with it. The *Los Angeles Times* had one article on it.

TRACY: Did you find carcasses or skeletons of animals?

TED: We found 2000 animal bones. We did not find any human bones. We had everything analyzed. It cost thousands of dollars. I spent personally $17,000 out of my pocket on that project, and then some of the companies that worked with us donated their time, and we had monetary donations from others. Anyway, I'm the guy that went in there and found the tunnels, so I'm not too popular with my adversaries. And yes, those kids identified some actors. One was Chuck Norris, whom they said was involved.

TRACY: So, do you think that's likely to be true, or do you think that's just something that they told the kids?

TED: Oh, I don't think there's any question that the kids were telling the truth. Because they [officials?] said that they were hallucinating, but the kids talked about tunnels under the school, they talked about being flown up into the mountains. Well, I know the abandoned Satanic site in Crestmount, I've got pictures of it. And I went up there and took pictures, and when the case broke I called Dale Reuben, the prosecutor, and I said, "I think I know where the kids were taken." She wasn't interested. Nobody wanted to look at it. And the kids said there were tunnels under the school. There *were* tunnels under the school--they'd been filled in, and I have a 186-page report by the archaeologists that documents it. This wasn't me going out and digging. I'm just an investigator. This was an archaeologist. This was a doctor from UCLA. We kicked their asses.

TRACY: So, do you think the prosecution in that case was being controlled?

TED: Yes, I do.

TRACY: And so this whole operation in the McMartin school was part of Project MONARCH?

TED: Yes, there's no question in my mind. I've been trying to do something about this for years, ever since I ran into it and discovered it. I even had my own radio talk show for two years.

TRACY: Oh, was that a national talk show?

TED: Yeah, it was all over the world, actually. It was short wave out of Nashville, WWCR, Worldwide Christian Radio. I've done probably a thousand radio shows myself. As you can tell I can talk right off the top of my head, and I have the documentation to back it up. "They"--meaning this evil element within our government-- they're very concerned about me, because I've got the documentation. I have it hidden in four different locations. I went on a ten-day trip a year ago last June, and, Hell, they came in here and stole a bunch of my boxes--somebody did. They didn't take any jewelry or anything like that, they just took my research. They're so concerned about the research I have that they don't know what to do about me. You know, and I don't back down to them, either.

TRACY: So you don't know specifically who it was that broke in?

TED: They didn't break in. They have keys for everything. They're professional burglars, professional killers, they're assassins; they're almost every evil word you can think of. That's what we're dealing with. And like I said, this involves our US intelligence community, the CIA in particular, and then later on the FBI, whereas in the past it didn't. There's no question about it. What they do is, the CIA recruits out of Special Forces. McVeigh came right out of Special Forces class. They recruit them out of there, and then they train them to be assassins and killers, and to run their drug operations. Now McVeigh wrote a letter to his sister, I don't know if you remember this or not. He said this in his letter. This is public information. So I'm not talking off the top of my head.

TRACY: Do you think that most of the cases you hear of Satanic Ritual Abuse are all parts of this government operation?

TED: Oh, I don't think there's any question that it's an organized ring, if that's what you're looking for. There is a conspiracy here. There's no question about that.

TRACY: And what's the overall goal?

TED: The overall goal is to take over the world.

TRACY: They just essentially want everyone to be mind-controlled slaves?

TED: They want to take over the world. They want a two-class society: the very rich, and then the slobs, like us, you now, the servants? It's well-planned, and it's well-organized, and if you look at the 25 goals that were set forth in 1776, 230-some years ago, you'll see that most of those, are about 85% complete today. Like corruption of the youth through sex and drugs. I mean, look at what's going on with our youth today. Control of the mainstream media. Do you think the mainstream media is going to have the guts to print what I'm telling you now? Hell, no. And I've got the documentation. I've got cabinets full of material, to prove that I'm right. Hell, no, they won't, because they've got the Brokaws, and the Rathers. You know, you've got those people. They're all being controlled. They wouldn't dare talk about this because they'd lose their jobs. Nor would the *Los Angeles Times*, or the *New York Times*. They won't touch any of this stuff. Maybe *Hustler Magazine* has the guts to print this, I don't know. Let me tell you a little hook, here. It's really interesting. One of the... Who's the owner of *Hustler*?

TRACY: Larry Flynt.

TED: Yeah, Larry Flynt's former body guard was at the time a contract killer, and attempted to take my life in 1987. His name was Bill Menser.

TRACY: What were the circumstances?

TED: Well, there was a fellow named Mike Riconosciuto from the CIA, who was talking, exposing these people. You see, when people come forward from the inside who can give direct knowledge of what's going on, they either end up dead or in prison. Well, Mike Riconosciuto started talking. He's in prison now for 30 years. But Mike and I worked together back in the early 80s, and we put five people in jail who were contract killers. One of them was Bill Menser. Menser was one of Flynt's bodyguards. A guy named Lamatta was another. And they were convicted of murdering a guy named Roy Raiton from Long Island, New York, along with Lani Jacobs. Jacobs, of course, was female, not working for Larry Flynt. Anyway, one of the people we put in jail was arranging for contract killings, and his name was Dr. John P. Nichols, out of Indio, California. And when he got out, he called Menser, and told Menser to do his job on me. I was able to avoid Menser, and Mike and I put Menser in jail. We went to the D.A. and told him all about his involvement in the Roy Raiton murder and everything. So anyway, Larry Flynt will know all about Menser, he'll know all about Lamatta, and a guy named Lowell was the one who drove the car that night when they killed Roy

Raiton. And that puts a little twist on this. Larry Flynt had people right in his midst who were involved in this. And Bill Menser was known as "Charles Manson II" in Hollywood. He's a killer.

TRACY: What do you think about JonBenet Ramsey?

TED: I have no documentation on that, but the scenario fits a Satanic cult ceremony.

TRACY: In that she was killed on Christmas night?

TED: Yeah, that's a big Satanic holiday.

TRACY: And Chandra Levy, too, disappeared on Walpurgis Night.

TED: She disappeared on May 1st, a big Communist holiday.

[*Editor's Note: She disappeared between April 30, Walpurgis Night, and May 1st, which is May Day. They are primarily pagan holidays, although May Day is a traditional protest day for Socialists.*]

TRACY: Would you speculate that Condit, then, is a controller as well?

TED: I have no idea, but from what I've read and seen, I wouldn't be surprised. But it definitely appears that he was involved in kinky sex, which of course, I guess, there's millions of people who are involved in that in this country and around the world.

TRACY: You heard that he specifically referred to his women as "sex slaves." [Source: *The Globe*.]

TED: Well, there you go. That's what they are, they're sex slaves.

TRACY: How do they go about programming these people?

TED: It's a combination of torture, hypnosis, drugs. And what happens is, they torture them so much, that their personality splits in order to endure the pain and misery. When their personality splits, they became another person, and it's through this technique that they train them. Then in training they make it so that they can give them a trigger word, say "green," or "red," or pick up the phone and call them. And they have an assignment to go out and do something--like, say, go out and do a hit, or something like that. That's kind of a layman's definition of it, but that's the way it works.

TRACY: Have you spoken to anyone who was a controller or programmer?

TED: Oh yeah, sure.

TRACY: And so they told you this as well?

TED: Oh yeah, I've got it from all kinds--I've got it 15 ways from Sunday. These people all talk like they're crazy, but there's so many of them, and they don't know each other, and their stories are the same, so there's got to be something to it.

TRACY: I've noticed that a lot of the women are really weird. Like Cathy O'Brien. She sounds like she's really smart, and she sounds like she knows a lot about the history of mind control, and all sorts of things. But then she'll use really inappropriate words in a sentence, and it just seems like there's a lot of common knowledge that she doesn't have. And a lot of these women are like this. So it does seem like they really have been isolated from society, and just grew up in the whole Satanic cult world with no exposure to real life.

TED: Well, half of them sound crazy, and the other half sound semi-crazy. But this is so prevalent, and it's from so many sources, that there's absolutely no question about it. By the way, I've got the Congressional reports where Congress investigated back in 1977. So, hey, Congress knows about it.

TRACY: They investigated MK-ULTRA, or Project MONARCH specifically?

TED: MK-ULTRA and Project MONARCH. Yeah, I've got all

this information. The reports are available. I've got all this information right back here in my little cabinet drawer some place.

TRACY: To what extent do you think people in the Federal government know about this?

TED: I think they know, but they're covering it up. They don't want to come forward with it. A lot of people do. I personally went back to Washington in 1986-1987, talked to some congressmen, senators, administrative assistants, and told them about this. Biden was one, Dan Coats out of Indiana, former congressman and senator, was another. And then I backed it up with documentation, with paper. So they know about it. I don't know why they won't come forward with it. First of all, it's unbelievable, and if you start talking about it, people will think you're crazy. But you know, hey, Congress investigated it, but it was basically not reported by the mainstream media again.

TRACY: How many people do you think there are out there who are mind control subjects?

TED: Well, O'Brien will tell you about 10 million, but I personally think it's between 3 and 4 million. And it's there. The grandmother in the McMartin case [Virginia McMartin] told one of the mothers that she travels all over the world and sets up these pre-schools. And Dr. Roland Sommit out of UCLA Hospital has made the statement that there are 50 other pre-schools in the country where the kids talk about tunnels under the school.

TRACY: Would you say it's just dangerous to send your kid to pre-school?

TED: It depends. You have to investigate it. Now, if the pre-school says: "OK, you cannot come here between the hours of nine and four, even if you're a parent," then that's Number One. You don't go there. You don't put your kid in that school. Because, why would they object to you coming in and checking on your kid, right? Then if the kid, let's say, had a little blood in the diapers, and so forth. We're talking about two, three, four-year old kids with a little blood in the diaper. You certainly don't want to send your kid back to that. Or if the kid doesn't want to go to school, listen to your child. I've got a checklist here of signs of what to look for with your kids. This goes on and on, and I can talk for hours on this.

TRACY: Have you heard of the supposed electrified cages full of babies at China Lake?

TED: No, I can't say that I've heard about that. But I have heard, you know, rumors that there are underground cities, and that some of these kids are being kept in those underground cities. Now Paul Bonacci in Omaha, Nebraska has made the statement that he was involved when he was 10-13 years old. He was used as a decoy in malls, and parks, and so forth, to attract kids that age, and then the adults grab them and run off with them. And Paul Bonacci received his training at Offutt Air Force Base. That's one of the military bases. And I tell you, it's kind of ironic, but Michael Aquino was at Fort Bragg at the time of the Geoffrey MacDonald murders that I talked about when I first started talking to you.

TRACY: Have you talked to Michael Aquino?

TED: No, I don't have anything to do with him. There's a guy named Craig Lockwood who has some phenomenal information about this. He can really fill you in. He wrote a book called *Other Alters*. It's all about the Satanic cult movement in this country, and it's about Michael Aquino. It's an interesting story. He told me that this sold 15,000 copies in just a couple of weeks. His publisher was really excited about it. Then all of the sudden he was sued in Minneapolis where the publisher is, and they found out that Michael Aquino went around and bought all of them out. Now you have to have a pretty good-sized network to do that. He bought all the books, and then sued the publisher, and also Craig. But Craig won the lawsuit.

TRACY: So that means the judge believed that this had actually taken place. And in the Presidio case [a sexual abuse case in which Aquino was accused], didn't the Army have to pay a substantial settlement to the parents of the kids?

TED: Yeah, I think they did. We had the thing in Westpoint, too, and there was a captain there who resigned his commission because of that, mostly 'cause it was a cover-up.

TRACY: I just remember something about a sexual harassment lawsuit. So that was part of Project MONARCH as well?

TED: Oh yeah. These pre-schools are, I believe, prep schools for these people to indoctrinate these kids and expose them to the Satanic movement.

TRACY: re some of these kids also raised in Satanic families, specifically for this purpose?

TED: Oh yeah. Of course. I talked to a woman who was sent to law school by them to study immigration laws. They would fly her Germany to bring kids back into this country. She'd drop them off, bring them in at Kennedy Airport, and turn them in to two men. Then she'd disappear, and go back and get another one.

TRACY: So are there physical or psychological traits that they look for in these kids? Do they choose kids specifically for reasons?

TED: No, I don't think so. One of that tactics that they use is, say I'm a perpetrator, or I'm a pedophile. I'll contact an individual who I know can arrange for the kids, and I'll say "OK, I want a 13-year-old boy or girl, whatever the case might be, blue-eyed, blond-haired." And then that person would go out and get pictures of about four or five kids surreptitiously, come back, show me the pictures. And I say, "Oh, I want this one." Then they go and kidnap the kid. Like an order, you know? It's like looking at a catalogue. "Oh, I'll take this coffee pot, or I'll take that automobile," or whatever the situation might be.

TRACY: Don't they also get a lot of kids at Disneyland?

TED: Yeah, they've quashed that, I understand. Kids have disappeared at Disneyland regularly. There are kids who've disappeared here in Las Vegas, and of course the officials are being very careful not to let that out to the public because this is a big entertainment center.

TRACY: And a lot of the slaves say that Disney imagery was part of their programming.

TED: Oh, absolutely. Everyone that I've talked to on the west coast had some training at Disneyland. I've talked to hundreds of them in the last 22 years. It's quite an elaborate operation. There has to be a central location, there has to be people in charge, it has to be organized, and hey, it's covered-up. The ones who are involved in this, you know, it's a secret who they are, and it's a secret what they do, but it does involve human sacrifices and Satanic ceremonies, period.

TRACY: Have you heard of Mormons being involved in this?

TED: Heavily involved in this. At the very top. I've got a whole paper on that. They did their own investigation in 1990 of it, and they came up with the same thing. I've got all the reports, by the way. That's just typical of my documentation.

TRACY: So they were investigating themselves, and they found evidence of human sacrifices?

TED: Well, they found evidence of Satanism, which would include human sacrifice.

TRACY: Does the police force ever investigate this?

TED: No. They don't touch it. There've been police officers who have tried to do something about it who have ended up dead, or they're re-assigned. These people are killers. We're not talking about nice people. And they'll stop at nothing to further their cause. Anybody who gets in their way is dead, or gets put in jail. I have a list of the leaders of the occult movement on the west coast, which is my insurance policy. If anything happens to me, that goes out to the public.

False Memories:
An Interview with Pamela Freyd

By Tracy R. Twyman

Pamela Freyd is the co-founder of the False Memory Syndrome Foundation. She founded the organization with her husband Peter Freyd in 1992 after their daughter Jennifer Freyd, a Professor of Psychology at the University of Oregon, accused Peter of abusing her sexually as a child, based on memories she had recovered through therapy. This interview took place on August 28, 2001.

TRACY: Is "False Memory Syndrome" (specifically related to memories of child sexual abuse) a relatively new phenomenon? If so, when do you think this problem first began, and what were the causal factors?

PAMELA: It's important to begin any discussion of the topic of false memories with the fact that all the mental health professional organizations have issued statements saying that the only way that one can distinguish a true from a false memory is through external corroboration.

We all have false memories but generally they don't make a huge difference in our lives. When such a memory leads to the accusation of criminal behavior of another person, however, the stakes are raised. To be falsely accused of the unforgivable crime of child sexual abuse places individuals in a quandary. How does anyone prove a negative?

The Foundation has done a number of surveys of the families that have made contact. One of the questions in a survey we are just now analyzing is "In what year did you learn about the accusation?" We have one person in 1970 and another in 1971 who said they were accused in those years based solely on the claim of a "recovered repressed memory" with no other external evidence. We have a total of 12 reports from the 1970--contrasted with more than 550 reports for just the years 1991-1992. The frequency data indicate that the recovered memory phenomenon is a fad--at least based on the data from the surveys. The numbers have been in decline since 1992.

The McMartin case in 1983 received national media attention and made child abuse and Satanic Ritual Abuse a front page topic. Sociologists have referred to the false memory/child abuse accusations phenomenon in terms of a "moral panic." Child abuse is inherently evil and as statistics about its frequency increased, so did fear. When people are afraid, they panic. That's why schools have fire drills so that students don't panic should there be a fire. People often get trampled in panics caused by fires and they get accused in moral panics.

The explosive period of the fad appears to have begun in 1987-1988. Whether it is a cause or an effect is not clear, but 1988 saw the publication of the book *The Courage to Heal* by Ellen Bass and Laura Davis. Since that book has been listed as the most recommended book by psychotherapists (at least in the early 90s) it is possible that it helped spread the beliefs.

TRACY: Could you estimate what percentage of "recovered" abuse memory claims investigated by your organization are found to be based on false memories?

PAMELA: The Foundation cannot determine the truth or falsity of an accusation in the absence of external corroboration anymore than anyone else can. Indeed, the Foundation would not be the appropriate group to conduct investigations since it could be said to be biased. The Foundation does not "certify" anyone but rather has as its purpose to disseminate information about the nature of memory. Individual families have tried to get mental health professionals to investigate the accusations and have filed complaints for that purpose. Because the accusers would not release any records, however, this approach did not work. Some families brought lawsuits in the hope that this would open an investigation, but again, without access to records, there is little that can be done. What is left then, are the cases in which a child sued and that case then went to court. Most of these types of cases have been dismissed for lack of evidence.

What the Foundation noted was that the reports from the people who made contact showed certain patterns, and it was these patterns that brought alarm to scientists and psychiatrists who studied memory. Therapists were using hypnosis, guided imagery, sodium amatol, relaxation exercise, participation in groups, reading suggestive literature and other techniques in an effort to excavate memories. Although people may remember things with any of these techniques, there is absolutely no evidence that what they remember is historically accurate. Indeed, because these are suggestive techniques, it is highly probably that the patients pick up the suggestion and create false memories.

It's important to remember how memory works. If it worked like a tape recorder, storing everything that was experienced, it would make sense to dig for memories because the problem would be one of access. But that is not how memory works. People store bits and pieces and even these bits and pieces can be lost and altered over time. When someone has a "memory" it is a highly creative process of reconstruction. The bits and pieces are woven together to make a story that makes sense to the person in the here and now. People fill in the blanks. They incorporate information from a variety of sources.

TRACY: What telltale signs do you look for to determine if a recovered memory is false? What would it take to convince your organization that a recovered memory was true?

PAMELA: I repeat what I wrote previously, the Foundation has no way of knowing whether a particular memory is true or false in the absence of external corroboration. If any of the suggestive techniques I mentioned previously are used (i.e., hypnosis, sodium amatol, guided imagery, relaxation exercises, participation in survivor groups, reading suggestive literature, seeing suggestive videos, etc.) the task becomes virtually impossible. Any memory that arises using such techniques must be suspect because of the suggestibility inherent in the use of the techniques themselves.

TRACY: Does your organization on the whole reject claims of childhood Satanic Ritual Abuse? Are there any cases of SRA that your organization has investigated which were not found to be the result of False Memory Syndrome?

PAMELA: Kenneth Lanning (1992) of the FBI investigated many cases and found no external corroboration for the types of claims to which you are referring. A much more extensive study was conducted by psychologist Gail Goodman and colleagues for the National Center on Child Abuse and Neglect (1994). They found no external corroboration for the many cases they examined. What they did find was that "a very small group of clinicians, each claiming to have treated scores of cases, accounted for most of the reports of ritualistic child abuse." In Great Britain, anthropologist La Fontaine (1994) examined all the cases of claimed Satanic Ritual Abuse (SRA) in that country and came up empty handed for evidence. She found that belief in SRA was closely linked to fundamentalist religious groups. In 1995, Bottoms, Shaver, Goodman and Qin examined whether religious beliefs can foster child abuse. They were alarmed at finding cases "involving the withholding of medical care for religious reasons, abuse related to attempts to rid a child of evil, and abuse perpetrated by persons with religious authority," and argued that as a society greater effort should be made to protect children in these circumstances.

Evidence for an intergenerational Satanic cult that breeds children that they then abuse does not seem to exist. Rebellious teens may dabble with Satanic symbols and ceremonies and there are religious groups that focus on Satan but there is no evidence for the kinds of claims made in books such as *Michelle Remembers*.

TRACY: I understand that 18% of the claims that you investigate involve some form of SRA. Can you speculate on why so many such claims have come forth since the 1980, all remarkably similar?

PAMELA: The McMartin case put SRA on the front page and into the minds of many people. I suspect that the similarity of the claims is due to the fact that books such as "Michelle Remembers" were quite popular and that authority was given to these beliefs by some television programs, both those that brought on "experts" and those that displayed patients who held such beliefs. Within the therapeutic community, ideas were spread at continuing education seminars. There are now, however, hundreds of former patients who, once they left the therapeutic context, came to realize that their memories of Satanic abuse were fantasy, although deeply disturbing and painful at the time of belief.

TRACY: Has your organization specifically investigated the claims of people whose recovered memories involve the so-called secret "Project MONARCH," supposedly the CIA's experimental program aimed at creating "mind-controlled sex slaves" and Manchurian Candidate-like assassins through the infliction of severe childhood trauma, along with the use of drugs and hypnosis?

PAMELA: No. The Foundation has limited its focus to issues of families torn apart based solely on claims of recovered repressed memories of childhood sexual abuse.

TRACY: According to both alleged victims of and self-proclaimed experts on Project MONARCH, the above-described techniques (including the use of rape, torture, and "Satanic Ritual Abuse") so traumatize the young mind of the victim that it splits off into numerous separate personalities, to compartmentalize the trauma. Each of these personalities can supposedly then be programmed to perform specific tasks without the knowledge of the others. These programs can purportedly be accessed later through the use of pre-arranged code-words and signals, which automatically trigger the hypnotic state in the victim. Does your organization have any opinion on whether or not such programming is even possible using the techniques described above?

PAMELA: The FMS Foundation has not been involved in examining any of the claims about CIA brainwashing. The purpose of the Foundation is to provide the public and professions with accurate information about memory and to help those families who contact the Foundation by providing information. I think the following passage by Philip Zimbardo and Susan Andersen addresses scientific understanding on the CIA mind-control topic:

> *"John Mark's (1979) expose of the CIA's secret mind-control program made it clear that no foolproof way of "brainwashing" another person has ever been found. (The*

word "brainwashing" is used here in its popular connotation, which came out of movies and sensationalized press accounts--that is, absolute control over another. This is not what the leading researchers [Lifton, 1961, Schein, Schneier, & Barker, 1961] of the Korean War-era "brainwashing" meant by their terms, thought reform and coercive persuasion, respectively.) Electroshock therapy, hypnosis, exquisite torture devices, and psychoactive drugs have not proved adequate for the task of reliably directing behavior through specific scenarios designated by would-be manipulators. It is a person (or various persons) in a convincing social situation–not gadgets or gimmicks–who control the minds of others. the more worried we are about being regarded as ignorant, uncultured, untalented, or boring, and the more ambiguous the events that must be evaluated, the more likely we are to take on the beliefs of those around us to avoid being rejected by them." (Michael D. Langone (Editor) Recovery from Cults: Help for Victims of Psychological and Spiritual Abuse, Norton, 1993, page 106.)

Although it has been often repeated that severe childhood trauma causes the mind to split and multiple personalities to develop, there is no scientific evidence to that effect. This notion spread after the publication of *Sybil*. In the last five years two things have occurred that cause grave doubt as to whether Sybil was actually a multiple personality. First was an interview with Herb Spiegel, M.D., one of the doctors who treated her. Spiegel said that Sybil was not MPD. Second was the discovery of some tapes of talks between the doctor and author who wrote the book *Sybil*. In these tapes, it appears that Sybil's MPD was created by these two.

That someone has the manifestations of MPD is not at issue; they may. The question is what is the cause of the symptoms. Many in the psychiatric community believe that MPD is iatrogenic, that is, caused by the use of hypnosis and the type of interviewing techniques of the doctor.

TRACY: Has your organization specifically investigated the claims of the following people:

- Brice Taylor (a.k.a. Susan Ford, author of *Thanks for the Memories: The Truth Has Set Me Free*?

- Cathy O'Brien (author of *The TRANCE Formation of America*)?

- Arizona Wilder (author, *Revelations of a Mother Goddess*)?

PAMELA: The FMS Foundation is not an investigative group. Its purpose is to provide information about the nature of memory as it has appeared in the scientific literature. There are hundreds, probably thousands, of stories that people have written about their recovered memories of torture of some sort--in past lives, in space alien abductions and in Satanic rituals. Evidence is lacking for the existence of these events--other than the stories. A case study or a story is not scientific evidence although it can be used as a basis to being a scientific program. When it comes to memory, the scientific program has been in place for many years, and what has been discovered is how suggestible people are.

A very well-known memoir is that of Binjamin Wilkomirski, who wrote of his childhood in German concentration camps (*Fragments*). The existence of the concentration camps is not an issue as is the existence of space alien abductions, past lives and intergenerational Satanic cults. The book received numerous prizes and he was given awards and spoke around the world. The publisher withdrew it in 1999 when it was discovered that the memoir was fiction. The author had spent the war years in Switzerland.

It's interesting how this ties in with Satanic Ritual Abuse. Credibility had been given to the Wilkomirski story when it was confirmed by a Laura Grabowski who claimed she had known Wilkomirski at Auschwitz. But in an interesting twist, it appears that Laura Grabowski was quite confused. Her real name is Lauren Stratford and she is the author of *Satan's Underground*, a book in which she describes being forced to be a "baby breeder" in a Satanic cult. An expose of Grabowski appeared in the Nov, 1999 *Cornerstone Magazine*. Lauren Statford was born in Tacoma, Washington, and has spent her entire life in the United States. *[Editor's note: According to Cornerstone's website,*

cornerstonemag.com, "Lauren Stratford doesnα exist, except as
the pen name of Laurel Rose Willson, and Satanα Underground is
only one of the stories sheα told about her life.м]

TRACY: Some high-profile and outspoken "child abuse
survivors" with recovered memories have also claimed to be
victims of "harassment" by the FMSF after coming forward with
their accusations. Does your organization engage in any contact
with the alleged victims that could be construed as such?

PAMELA: The only persons I know who might fit your
description are David Calof and Laura Brown, Ph.D. They are both
therapists rather than survivors and have both complained about
being picketed by Chuck Noah, a retired construction worker in
Seattle, Washington. One look at the names on the Scientific
Advisory Board of the FMS Foundation should belie any idea that
the Foundation is interested in picketing as a way to educate
people about the nature of memory. The Foundation has held
conferences and seminars. And indeed a number of these were
picketed by people opposed to the Foundation. The Foundation is
interested in fostering family reconciliation where it is possible,
not in harming anyone.

I cannot answer your question unless you tell me what you are
referring to. What harassment? Who? When? In the same manner,
I might ask if you have stopped beating your husband or
whomever. How does one respond to such insinuations?

TRACY: Is the term "False Memory Syndrome" recognized by
the psychiatric field at large?

PAMELA: The term is now in most dictionaries and even in the
OED. To my knowledge no one has sought to have it included in
the "Diagnostic and Statistical Manual" of the American
Psychiatric Association. The foundation is interested in promoting
therapy in which the development of false memories is not a likely
outcome. Did PTSD exist before it was included in the DSM? Did
MPD exist before inclusion in the DSM? Since there have been at

least a dozen professional mental health journal issues devoted to the topic of false memories, I must assume that it is recognized at some level by professionals.

TRACY: Is there any difference between a false memory and outright lying?

PAMELA: A lie is a deliberate falsification often for some purpose. People with false memories believe them sincerely and with much conviction, especially if some hypnotic techniques are involved. There is a difference.

Postscript:
Satanic Ritual Abuse and Sex Slavery in the New Millennium

By Tracy R. Twyman

I have a little bit of experience with "Satanic Panic." When I was 14 years old and living two doors up from my best friend in the small town of Sherwood, Oregon, I got exposed to it first-hand. I already had a reputation for having a "dark" personality in my high school. I was into Goth music, I wore black clothes, and I sometimes read books about the occult. My friend, who also listened to Goth music and wore dark clothes, had recently begun to develop a similar reputation. One day my friend's aunt came into town to visit his family, and brought with her a set of documentary videos made by an Evangelical church group about Satanism. She showed the videos to my friend's parents. By the end of the day, they were convinced that their son was a Satanist, and that he was possessed by demons. They held a group prayer ritual in the living room with the aim of removing the demonic influence from the house.

Shortly after this happened, my friend had a fight with his parents about an unclean bedroom that resulted in him being committed as an in-patient at a local mental hospital, where counselors repeatedly tried to get him to confess some deep secret of personal shame. He had no idea why his parents had done this to him or what the counselors were after, but within a week he was released. When he returned home, he found that all of his Goth CDs and most of his clothes had been burned in a bonfire in his backyard by his parents. Next, he was taken to see a Christian counselor from his parents' church, who presented him with a list of addresses that had been found in his bedroom. My friend recognized them as a list of record stores in downtown Portland that he had drawn up last time he went shopping for music. The counselor asked if these were the locations of his "Satanic meetings," and even presented surveillance photographs taken from outside of these establishments. This was the first time my friend realized that his parents and their church had launched an investigation with the aim of proving that he belonged to a Satanic cult.

Within a couple of weeks, I too found myself at the center of an investigation. Counselors at school began quizzing me frequently, and even brought my parents in for an interview. They never did say what they were investigating me for, but the endless suspicion and questioning caused me to drop out of school and take up instead at a local community college. At this time the landlord of the house where I lived unexpectedly reneged on our lease agreement, and my family was forced to move.

Later my friend also dropped out and joined me at the college. We moved on with our lives and forgot about the whole thing. It wasn't until two years later that a slip of the tongue from my friend's grandmother revealed some of the context of what had happened. Apparently, his parents (who raised sheep on a farm) had discovered one of their sheep brutally butchered in the barn. They leapt to the obvious conclusion: "Our son and his friend Tracy must have done it! They must belong to a Satanic cult! Tracy is probably the high priestess!" They even had enough imagination to conclude that their son had probably blocked out the traumatic memory of committing the sacrifice, and would need to be committed to a mental hospital so that his memories could be recovered.

According to my friend's grandmother, his parents had gone to the school principal and the local police with their suspicions. They had even accused my parents of being involved, and said that we had a "Satanic star" hanging in our living room window (which was actually a sun catcher shaped like a sun with a smiley face). His grandmother said that the police had actually tapped my phone looking for proof that we had butchered the sheep, but found none.

I suppose as a teenager I didn't have that much of a reputation to ruin, but my parents did, and it seems they may have been forced to move out of their house because of this smear. If it is true that my phone was tapped by the police, that compounds the injustice a hundred time. What gave these people the right to try to ruin our lives with their baseless accusations? How dumb did the police and school counselors have to be to go along with it? Is suspicion of "Satanism" really enough to justify locking up a kid up in a mental hospital against his will? There is one more nagging question: who killed the sheep anyway?

I have no doubt that this experience caused my interest in occultism, which before had been no more than a fashion statement, to flourish into a serious study. When I grew up and became an occult writer, even writing about conspiracy theories involving the "Satanic Illuminati," I found myself being accused by other writers of involvement in the conspiracy. I found conspiracy flow charts on the internet linking me and my acquaintances to the Trilateral Commission and the Bilderberg Group. This time, though, I understood the hysteria, and found it more humorous than threatening.

Still, having been on the receiving end of these accusations, you may wonder why I have written and published so much information about so-called Project MONARCH. Many researchers think that stories of Satanic Ritual Abuse are urban legends, and those who claim to be victims are smearing those they accuse just as I have been smeared in the past. Certainly I know from experience how easily this can happen. But I also now know first-hand a great deal about secret societies, and the types of people who are typically drawn to join occult groups. While this is only a stereotype, it is not uncommon to find that these people have symptoms of megalomania, socio-pathology, sadism, sexual deviance, an attraction to evil, and a willingness to do anything that they think will help them to acquire more power. I know that many occult rituals do involve bizarre sex acts, and sometimes blood sacrifice. Some occultists include their own young children in rites and practices which may be remembered by them as unpleasant or frightening. For sure, the same thing can be said about religious zealots of any stripe, but occultists are no exception. There is also certainly a confluence between the membership of certain occult groups, and involvement in things like government, intelligence, high finance, and organized crime. Most definitely, many occult groups use techniques on their membership that can only be called "mind control," and intelligence agencies have been experimenting with mind control for many decades now.

Furthermore, we know that the statistics on human trafficking in our modern world are horrifyingly huge, as are the statistics on missing and abused children. It is estimated that 27 million people are currently enslaved today, most of them as sex slaves. The State Department says that somewhere between 600,000 and 800,000 people are illegally trafficked across borders throughout the world. 70% of these are female and 50% are children. The *"vast majority,"* they say, end up in the sex trade. This puts an entirely different spin on the subject of illegal immigration across the Mexican border. We talk about issues of racism and depressed wages, but it seems there is a much more important issue at stake when you consider that so many of those crossing the border, according to our own government, are not just working family people seeking a better life, but rather unfortunate victims of the human sex trade. We know that the Mexican border is purposely left porous, and illegal alien criminals are routinely set free from jail to offend again, for reasons of political expediency. But perhaps the lax border issue is connected to something more than the courting of the Latino vote.

Another thing we know about the sex slave industry is that it is incredibly cruel and sadistic. Because of its underground nature, it is impossible to estimate numbers accurately, but from the evidence and eyewitness testimonies we do have, we know that sex slaves are not only repeatedly raped, but beaten, tortured, and eventually killed. Often this abuse is perpetrated merely for sexual pleasure by sadistic people, and sometimes it is captured on film to be sold to a sick audience always hungry for more. Some of this is also part of the conditioning of the slave: breaking down their will power for purposes of mind control. There is no doubt that the principles of Stockholm Syndrome (also known as Tauma-Bonding) and Dissociative Identity Disorder are being purposely studied and utilized by these slaves' handlers. They also know who to pay off in order to ensure that government officials look the other way. Sexual favors from slaves are often used for these pay-offs, and the proceedings are secretly filmed for future blackmail. There is no doubt that sex slavery could not exist without complicity from people in governments all over the world, including our own.

But what evidence is there of a global confluence of Satanism, sex slavery, and intelligence agencies as posited by the Project MONARCH stories? Most of that evidence has come from the testimonies of the people featured in this book, and much of it is hearsay. You can take it for what it's worth. However, I have noticed that since I wrote the original "Stepford Whores" article for *Hustler* in 2001 (included in this book), a number of cases have popped up in the news that seem to bear the earmarks of the same phenomena detailed in this book.

For instance, the latest Michael Jackson child molestation case made me suspicious as detailed rumors that started pouring during the trial. According to the stories, Jackson had for many years been bringing 12-to-14-year-old boys to his circus-like Neverland Ranch in California, showering them with toys and gifts, plying them with alcohol ("Jesus Juice," or wine in a Coke can), and sexually molesting them. In many cases, the parents of the boys seemed to be complicit in what was going on, as they repeatedly brought their sons to spend the night alone in bed with this strange grown man. Perhaps not coincidentally, Jackson reportedly showered the parents with gifts as well, including large sums of cash.

Friends of Jackson have reported his tendency to slip into child-like characters that seem like alternate personalities, his favorite being Peter Pan, "because he never has to grow up." He seems to be obsessed with the concept of wearing masks, and transmogrification, as demonstrated in the videos for his songs "Thriller" and "Black or White." This desire to transform himself has obviously led to Jackson's disastrous plastic surgery, and presumably ties in with the fact that he forces his children to wear masks while they are in public. Indeed, viewers of Martin Bashir's famous 2003 documentary exposé of Michael Jackson saw that he appeared to live in a 24-hour fantasy world of his own making in which he pretended to be a child. He shows all the signs of someone suffering from Dissociative Identity Disorder.

Jackson also shows the signs of having been sexually abused as a child, and indeed has accused his father Joseph of abusing him, as has his sister LaToya. Michael is known to have had psycho-sexual problems since early on. His highly-publicized marriage to Lisa Marie Presley is believed to have been a publicity stunt, while his marriage to Deborah Rowe was part of a scheme in which his first two children were produced through *in vitro* fertilization. They divorced in 1999, and Jackson had another child in 2002, but nobody knows who the mother is. The kids have always had their faces covered when shown in public. Some say this is partly because he is hiding the fact that they are obviously not his biological children.

So who are these kids, and what is happening to them in Michael Jackson's custody? We may never know, as Jackson was acquitted of the molestation charges, and immediately went running to Bahrain, a known child prostitution center where pedophilia is openly tolerated. The question of the children's safety becomes even more paramount when we consider allegations made by Jack Gordon, the former husband of Michael Jackson's sister LaToya, who claimed in a tell-all book to have witnessed Jackson sacrificing monkeys in occult rituals, and physically abusing his pet monkeys on several occasions. In a similar vein, *Vanity Fair* reported in March 2003 that in 2000 Michael Jackson paid a voodoo witchdoctor in Mali $150,000 to put a curse on his 24 most-hated enemies, including Steven Spielberg and David Geffen. The ceremony, which reportedly took place in Switzerland, required Jackson to bathe in the blood of 42 freshly-sacrificed cows.

Was Michael Jackson a Project MONARCH victim as a child? It has been said that the CIA's MK-ULTRA targeted members of the entertainment industry, and that many famous child actors and singers were in fact mind-controlled slaves. The name of his ranch, Neverland, as well as his obsession with Peter Pan, are suspicious, for as we know, this imagery was allegedly used as a programming base for MONARCH children, according to Cathy O'Brien. And what shape could you once see from the air when you fly over Neverland Ranch, made out of colorful flowers and bushes? The image of a Monarch butterfly.

Want another example? Take the case of the Hosanna Church in Ponchatoula, Louisiana. In May of 2005, police in the Tangipahoa Parish Sheriff's Office had just begun to investigate claims by a woman who said her children had been sexually abused by people at the church. All of the sudden the pastor of the church, Louis LaMonica, walked into the station unsummoned and offered to help them with their investigation. A quote from a *New York Times* article from May 25, 2005 explains what unfolded next:

> *"Mr. Lamonica, 45, matter-of-factly told them of having sex with at least two boys, from the time they were 4 until they were 12 or 13, as well as having sex with a dog, Mr. Carpenter said, adding that Mr. Lamonica did not act as though he was confessing to crimes. He was just trying to be helpful."*

Another article from the Associated Press from June 11, 2005 reveals what had seemingly been going on for the last several years. Witnesses described Satanic rituals in which cats were sacrificed, and "as many as two dozen" children of all ages were raped and/or molested, the cat blood being poured onto their naked bodies. In several instances, children were allegedly made to have sex with dogs. Physical evidence that was found at the church included ceremonial robes and the residue of pentagrams painted on the floor.

Why did Louis Lamonica walk into the sheriff's office and start confessing all of these things, apparently not thinking that he would get in trouble? Did he have some reason to suspect that the police would be sympathetic to him? It is one of the greatest mysteries of this case. At any rate, it only became more bizarre when lawyers for Lamonica's co-defendants (many of whom had already signed confessions) claimed that their clients were innocent by reason of "brainwashing." They said that an influential member of the church, not Lamonica, had used powers of persuasion to get these people to sign their confessions. The alleged motive for this was never explained. But many other members of the church continued to testify that the abuse did in fact occur. An article from November 29, 2007 in the *Hammond*

Star reported from the trial about one of the witnesses, married to one of the accused and mother to one of the alleged victims:

> *"Monica said that when she asked [her husband] why he was sexually abusing his own daughter, he said he wanted to make her 'non-human,' or nothing more than an object of his pleasure."*

The Hosanna Church trial is still ongoing as of this writing. In February of 2008 Louis Lamonica requested that the trial be moved to a new location, a motion that is currently still being considered.

Of course, many alleged cases of Satanic Ritual Abuse are supposed to have taken place in churches and religious institutions that use Christianity as a cover. Certainly there have been many real cases of children that were sexually abused in church, most notably by Catholic priests. William H. Kennedy has written an excellent book on the subject that links the phenomena of priest sex abuse to Satanism. It is called *Lucifer's Lodge: Satanic Ritual Abuse in the Catholic Church*. In it Kennedy reveals that many high-profile priest abuse cases contained Satanic and occult aspects that were ignored by the mainstream media. Among these is the case of Father Paul Shanley, an accused child-molesting priest who is linked with the founding of pro-pedophile group NAMBLA (the National Man-Boy Love Association), and with the Satan-worshipping Process Church of the Final Judgment. The latter has been connected by some writers to a series of ritualistic murders all over the United States, and former members claim they were involved in the trafficking of child pornography, including snuff films.

The existence of a snuff film industry is something that is denied by some researchers, who believe that it is merely an urban legend. They say that all alleged snuff films that have come to the attention of investigators turned out to be fakes. However, other investigators who have seen the same films disagreed. A film called *Snuff* that was purported to be the real thing was famously released in 1977, but the production company (ironically called "Monarch Films") admitted it was fake when threatened with prosecution. This famous incident appears to be in large part the basis of the argument that snuff films are merely "urban legend." But the fact is, we know that all over the world children are kidnapped, sexually abused and tortured, used in pornographic films, and murdered every single day. The odds that all of these things might have at least once *happened at the same time*--child rape, torture and murder caught on film and illegally distributed-- seem likely to be high. Some believe it is worse than this--that snuff films are indeed an integral part of the child porn industry. Supposedly they are available only to the highest rollers, with the buyers paying anything between $5,000 and $40,000 for a custom-made limited edition film production.

A great deal of information about alleged snuff films came out with the trial and investigation of Belgian serial child murderer Marc Dutroux. The Dutroux case was one that I was unfortunately not aware of at the time I wrote the article for *Hustler*, but it indeed matches up with many of the elements of the Project MONARCH stories contained in this book. Dutroux and his wife Michelle Martin had already been convicted of kidnapping and raping five girls in the 1980s (they had spent no more than three years in prison for their offenses) when in 1996, two missing young girls were found in the torture chamber secretly concealed within their basement. They also found the bodies of four other girls between the ages of 8 and 19, two of them starved to death (apparently by accident) as well as that of an adult accomplice, who was killed for failing to feed the two starved girls. All of the girls had been viciously raped and tortured repeatedly during their time in Dutroux's basement.

During the investigation and trial that followed, it was revealed that police had on many occasions failed to follow up on evidence that would have caught Dutroux much earlier, and possibly could have saved the lives of the girls. Several witnesses, including Dutroux's own mother, had reported to police their suspicions that he was connected to the disappearances of several local girls. Dutroux's house had been under police surveillance for this very reason when he took two girls out of his house to have them murdered, and later brought in two more to lock in his dungeon. Police supposedly had not noticed any of this while they were watching his house. They also failed to hear the screams of the girls locked in the basement when they searched Dutroux's house in 1995, after he had been arrested for car theft, for which he spent three months in jail. It was during this time that those girls starved to death.

The police incompetence did not cease after the arrest. Indeed, the original state prosecutor of the case complained of obstruction of his investigation from every level of government. Several witnesses came forth after Dutroux's arrest, alleging that they had been abused by him and others as part of a Satanic child prostitution and pornography ring that dealt in extreme torture and snuff films. These witnesses also said that clients of the ring included some of Belgium's most prominent politicians and businessmen, as well as members of Belgium's royal family. Dutroux himself confirmed all of this and more with his own testimony and statements to reporters. He admitted that he was part of a child porn and snuff film ring, and claimed that powerful elements in Belgium did not want his true story to be told. The prosecutor was taken off the case prematurely, a move that prompted an unprecedented outcry from the outraged Belgian public. 300,000 of them marched in Brussels to express their anger. Nonetheless, the case continued to be handled by a prosecutor and investigators who were now uninterested in following the leads in the case connecting Dutroux to any larger network, especially ones which included important members of the Belgian aristocracy.

But some unpleasant information about that aristocracy did surface in the wake of the Dutroux trial, and that is the existence of "pink ballets"--kinky top secret sex parties attended by the well-to-do of Belgium. Here is a quote from

the UK's *Telegraph* from March 16, 1997:

> *"Punch-drunk Belgium is reeling from a new shock after a senior police officer confirmed last week what has long been rumoured: that some of the country's leaders indulge in sex parties, known ironically as 'ballets roses.'*

It is a world of outwardly respectable private clubs in discreet suburbs of Brussels, Antwerp and Liège, but where, on arrival, members remove not just their coats, but their tops, bottoms and underwear as well."

The article also stated that the "ballets" may be a method used by organized criminals to compromise powerful people in government:

"Hugo Coveliers, a Belgian senator, argues that the 'ballets roses' are not independent of one another, but part of a system 'which operates to this day and is used to blackmail the highly placed people who take part.'"

More recently, Portugal is reeling from its own shocking revelations about powerful people and pedophilia. In October of 2007, the UK's *Daily Mail* ran a story about an orphanage in Lisbon called "Casa Pia" ("House of the Pious")) -- a state-run network of homes caring for upwards of 4,000 children -- where kids were regularly taken away in a van and pimped out to a high society pedophile ring. These children were allegedly taken repeatedly to the homes of "some of the leading members of Lisbon society--ranging from Portuguese government ministers and high-ranking diplomats, to famous television stars and members of the judiciary." They were drugged and raped. Much of it was filmed. Videos of some of these attacks were found in a child porn raid in Paris.

As in the case of Marc Dutroux in Belgium, the police in Portugal have been incompetent to the point where it almost seems like they're doing it on purpose. There was actually photographic evidence showing the alleged ringleader of the pedophile group and the victim children in the same room with some of the accused politicians, but the police "accidentally" lost these photos. That was in 1982, when the allegations first surfaced. Nothing was done and the abuse at Casa Pia continued. It took the filing of many more police reports over the next eleven years before arrests were made in 2003. The investigation led to the discovery four children who had been abducted from Casa Pia and imprisoned in the home of a Portuguese ambassador, as well as photographic evidence of the abuse. The accused ringleader, Carlos Silvino, has been quoted as saying he does not fear prosecution because, "They can't touch me--there are too many people involved."

A similar case that is breaking just at the time of this writing is that of the Haut de la Garenne, a youth hostel in Saint Martin, Jersey, in the Channel Islands that from 1867 to 1998 had been a home for orphaned and/or wayward children. In 2006 Haut de la Garenne became the center of an investigation into an alleged child abuse and pedophilia network operating on the isle of Jersey. Over 150 people claim to have been abused, in many cases by respected members of the Jersey establishment, and say that Haut de la Garenne was one of the main locations where abuse took place. Some claim to have been taken there specifically for abuse by their abusers. However, most of the victims were actual residents of the children's home and claim to have been abused by the staff there. Victims describe the abuse as systematic and part of the institution, occurring on an almost nightly basis. It often took place in a "secret basement" beneath the school.

It was this basement that was of special interest during the investigation, for when police visited the building with sniffer dogs, they found the secret basement, beneath a set of stairs. In there they discovered the remains of a very young child, still unidentified as I write this. They believe the child died in the 1980s and do not yet have an explanation as to why the body was hidden there. Shackles were also discovered there that had once been fastened to the wall. Police subsequently discovered another secret chamber, where the sniffer dogs indicated the presence of even more remains, but nothing tangible has been discovered as of yet.

Even if the child's death was somehow natural or accidental, why was it hidden in this manner? How could the staff of a children's home get away with something like that? Articles in the UK's *Guardian* newspaper describe a "culture of secrecy" on the island, where respected members of society all stick up for each other, while police and courts systematically ignore any accusations made against them, and obstruct any investigations made by outsiders. Even those former residents of Haut de la

Garenne who do not have tales of sex abuse to tell still say that there was non-stop physical and psychological abuse against all of the child residents, even through the 1980s. Nobody who knows the place finds it hard to believe that children were raped and murdered there.

During the recent investigation an even more disturbing connection was found. It was discovered that the Haut de la Garenne was connected to one of the UK's most notorious serial rapists: Edward Paisnel, also known as "the Beast of Jersey." From 1957 to 1971, Jersey was terrorized by an unknown assailant who broke into homes and raped children at night. He wore a bizarre costume that included a jacket studded with nails, a wig, and a bizarre rubber mask that made him look like a zombie. Police finally arrested him in 1971, still in this costume, fresh from the latest attack. When asked by the arresting officer why he was wearing such unusual attire, he replied, "I belong to a secret religious society. I'm on my way to a sex orgy."

This indeed would be Paisnel's defense. He claimed he had no connection to the rapes. He was merely a member of a black magic society where the membership was anonymous, and that they all wore masks to the meetings so that they couldn't recognize each other during normal life. When police searched his home they found a secret room, and altar covered with ritual items, as well as a number of books on occultism. During the trial it came out that he believed himself to be a reincarnation of Gilles de Rais, a notorious serial rapist and murderer from the 15th century who had once fought alongside Joan of Arc. He was convicted of raping, murdering and dismembering over 200 children, all as part of Devil worship rituals intended to bring forth the "Philosopher's Stone" that would allow him to turn lead into gold. However, Paisnel still maintained his innocence. But he was convicted, and died in prison in 1994.

The connection to Haut de la Garenne is a bizarre one. Until his arrest, Paisnel had actually visited the children's home every year at Christmas time … dressed as Santa Claus!

Since I wrote the "Stepford Whores" article for *Hustler* in

2001, there have been a few developments in the cases I discussed therein, most notably with that of the missing paper boy Johnny Gosch. In January 2005 a scandal broke out when a reporter working in the White House press room was found to be using a fake name. Calling himself "Jeff Gannon," the name on his driver's license was actually James Guckert. He was investigated in the first place because other White House reporters felt that he had been asking the President preferential questions, and thought it odd that they did not recognize him at all. The news outfit he worked for turned out to be Talon News, an internet operation, which caused many "real" print journalists resentment. Furthermore, upon researching his background it was learned that prior to his work for Talon News, Gannon/Guckert had been self-employed as a male prostitute who advertised his services online. Gannon lost his White House press pass, and Bush claimed to know nothing about him, while Democrats accused Gannon of being a White House plant meant to set up the President with softball questions at press conferences. They also took great joy in pointing out Gannon's prostitute past, mainly expressing shock that a gay man could be a Republican. Gannon continued his work in conservative journalism with his blog.

Had it not been for Noreen Gosch, the whole incident would have been forgotten. But in April 2005, Ms. Gosch did an interview with an alternative newsweekly in Des Moines, Iowa named *Pointblank* in which she stated that she believed Jeff Gannon was none other than her own missing son, Johnny Gosch. You will recall that Ms. Gosch claims to have been visited by Johnny as an adult in 1997, for one night only, in which he told her that he had been kidnapped by a Satanic child prostitution ring, and was now on the run from them. He left the next morning and continued running, never to be seen again. But now Ms. Gosch was saying that Gannon looked like the adult Johnny who had come to visit her. Furthermore, certain theories proffered by her friends John DeCamp and Ted Gunderson tended to back up this idea, she said. Within 24 hours of running the article, *Pointblank* was put out of business, and all the employees were put out of a job. The owners started a new paper that they began publishing the following week. Of course, many believe that *Pointblank* was killed because they ran the Gosch/Gannon story.

The "evidence" linking Gannon and Gosch is circumstantial at best, or at worst, the product of a fruitful imagination. First, some of Ted Gunderson's informants claim to know for sure that Gannon is Gosch: one is a confidential informant, the other is photographer Rusty Nelson, discussed in the interview with Gunderson in this book. Secondly, Johnny Gosch, Jeff Gannon, and the name on Jeff Gannon's driver's license, "James Guckert," all have the same initials: JG. Nothing is known about what happened to Johnny Gosch after he disappeared. Little can be established about the early life of Jeff Gannon, mainly because he chooses to keep it private. Gannon claims to be in his forties, about ten years older than Johnny Gosch would be today. But his prostitute websites claimed that he was ten years younger. Also, *if you think about it*, a boy who had been repeatedly raped and brainwashed by powerful Satanist pedophile politicians as part of a military/intelligence mind control program *might conceivably* grow up to be a gay prostitute with a flair for military clothing and a sympathy for Republican politics (he was supposedly brainwashed, remember?) As an adult, then, he might still be serving his handlers, making himself useful and thus keeping himself alive.

Another Gunderson informant, Paul Bonacci says that as a child victim of Project MONARCH (where he supposedly got to know Johnny Gosch very well), he was forced to participate in the production of a snuff film in which another boy was killed. He says that the man who filmed it was none other than gonzo journalist Hunter S. Thompson! This ties in, says Gunderson, because Thompson killed himself on February 21, 2005. Gunderson and others think Thompson was either murdered or killed himself because it was feared that with Jeff Gannon (possibly Johnny Gosch) now in the media spotlight, it was only a matter of time before Thompson's (alleged) involvement with child porn and snuff films was exposed. A few days later Rusty Nelson, who had been out of prison for many years, was suddenly arrested for failing to register as a sex offender in a town in which he no longer lived. Gunderson believes this was a warning from the evil cabal, warning to Nelson to keep his mouth shut about

Gannon, Gosch and Hunter S. Thompson. Another person who got arrested for child sex abuse right around this time was Paul Bishop, the self-proclaimed "CIA agent" who, according to her testimony, pretended to help Noreen Gosch search for her son in the early years before vanishing without a trace in 1985. Noreen didn't hear anything about him again until twenty years later, when she found out about his arrest.

While his White House press room scandal was rocking Washington that February, Jeff Gannon published a couple of articles with interesting titles. One was "Hiding in Plain Sight." While the article was about something else entirely, Gunderson and others think the title was a wink and nod by Gannon to those who were beginning to catch on to his true identity. Another article by Gannon on his blog, titled "Fear and Loathing in the Press Room," is believed to be a covert acknowledgement of the connection to Hunter S. Thompson, who famously wrote *Fear and Loathing in Las Vegas*.

However, to the contrary, in public Gannon's only acknowledgement of the allegations connecting him to Johnny Gosch has been complete denial. He has sent legal threats to Noreen Gosch and anyone else professing the theory. He has called in to radio talk shows where the theory was being discussed, issuing the same threats and denials. Then most recently in early 2007, he did the rounds of several cable television news programs denying any connection, and offering to take a DNA test to prove it. As of this writing, this has not actually happened yet, for reasons unknown.

This most recent wave of media activity happened just after another such wave also connected to the Johnny Gosch story. Noreen Gosch had gone on several television news shows asking for information from the public after she received a bunch of photographs from an anonymous source showing boys bound and gagged. She said that one of the boys in the photo was Johnny, and that it had been taken around the time that he was kidnapped. She wanted help identifying the other boys, and, if possible, the location in which the picture had been taken. A few weeks later, the boys in the photograph (now adults) came forward, and none of them were Johnny. The photographer also came forward, and he said that the pictures had been taken many years ago, when he and some younger friends were horsing around. They were not photos of kidnapped children, in other words. If Jeff Gannon does take a DNA test and proves that he is not Johnny Gosch, then that means that Noreen has twice now claimed that someone was her son when they in fact were not.

In February 2008, just as this book was about to go to press, Noreen Gosch published yet another photo on her website of a boy bound and gagged, which she claimed was her son, and which she claimed to have received from an anonymous source. She asked for the public's help in identifying the camp advertised on a camp bag sitting on the floor in the photograph. The bag says "Camp Caribou" quite clearly, and it is uncertain why she would need the public's help identifying it. A simple web search reveals that Camp Caribou is a Roman Catholic summer camp for boys in Maine. This photo has of course fueled internet speculation that the camp is a playground for pedophiles, with no other evidence surfacing as yet at the time of this writing.

As this book is being published, the topic of Project MONARCH is experiencing a popular resurgence on the internet, making the rounds on various left wing blogs and discussion forums, where supporters of Barack Obama are circulating the stories in an effort to connect Hillary Clinton to various evil deeds. New mind control and Satanic Ritual Abuse stories are popping up all the time. The latest headline turned up on The Drudge Report in early March 2008, although it was actually a story from November 2007. The mayor of the town of Centerton, Arkansas, known to his constituents as Ken Williams, suddenly resigned, announcing that his real name was "Don LaRose." He said that thirty years earlier, he had been kidnapped and brainwashed by Satanists. When he escaped from their clutches, he disappeared, leaving his wife and family, and taking on the name of another man who had died in an auto accident. He chose to resign his position as mayor when he was discovered by his abandoned family, although he did not choose to return to them, or to againtake up his former name.

Truly, reality is stranger than fiction, and a lot scarier.

Bibliography

"Belgians shocked by tales of secret policemen's orgy," by Marcus Warren, *Telegraph*, March 16, 1997.

"Beyond the Dutroux Affair: The reality of protected child abuse and snuff networks," by Joël van der Reijden, Project for the Exposure of Hidden Institutions, www.pehi.eu, July 25, 2007.

"Body found amid fears of child abuse ring on Jersey", by Sadie Gray, *The Independent*, February 24, 2008

"Hosanna case: Defendant's ex-wife testifies," by Don Ellzey, *Hammond Star*, November 29, 2007.

"Louisiana church hid dark secret, officials say," by Alan Sayre, Associated Press, June 11, 2005.

Lucifer's Lodge: Satanic Ritual Abuse in the Catholic Church, by William H. Kennedy, Reviviscimus, 2004.

"Mayor Resigns, Claims Abduction By Satan Worshippers," 4029tv.com, November 21, 2007.

National Crime Victims' Rights Week: Justice Isn't Served Until Crime Victims Are, U.S. State Department, www.ojp.usdoj.gov, April 10, 2005.

"Regina Louf's testimony," BBC News, Thursday, 2 May, 2002.

"Sex Charges Follow a Church's Collapse," By Rick Lyman , *New York Times*, May 25, 2005.

"*Vanity Fair* writer recounts Jacko voodoo story," CNN.comWednesday, March 5, 2003.

"Why Portugal is a haven for paedophiles--the disturbing backcloth to the Madeleine case," by Andrew Malone and Vanessa Allen, Daily Mail, October 20, 2007.

Mind Control Survivors' Testimony at the Human Radiation Experiments Hearings

(March, 1995)

Hearting Spokeperson: Forgive me if I am not pronouncing these names correctly ... we have Ms. Chris Denicola, Ms. Valerie Wolf, and Ms. Claudia Mullen. Are you all of New Orleans?

CVC: Yes.

HS: Thank you for making the effort to come up and speak to us.

Valerie Wolf: I am going to start. My name is Valerie Wolf. In listening to the testimony today, it all sounds really familiar. I am here to talk about a possible link between radiation and mind control experimentation that began in the late 1940's. The main reason that mind control research is being mentioned is because people are alleging that they were exposed as children to mind control, radiation, and chemical experimentation which were administered by the same doctors who were known to be involved in conducting both radiation and mind control research. Written documentation has been provided revealing the names of people, and the names of research projects in statements from people across the country. It is also important to understand mind control techniques and follow-ups into adulthood may have been used to intimidate particular research subjects into not talking about their victimization in government research. As a therapist for the past twenty-two years, I have specialized in treating victims and perpetrators of trauma, and their families. When word got out that I was appearing at this hearing, nearly forty therapists across the country (and I had about a week and a half to prepare) contacted me to talk about clients who had reported being subjected to radiation and mind control experiments. The consistency of people's stories about the purpose of the mind control and pain induction techniques, such as electric shock, use of hallucinogens, sensory deprivation, hypnosis, dislocation of limbs, and sexual abuse is remarkable.

There is almost nothing published on this aspect of mind control abuse with children, and these clients come from all over the country having had no contact with each other. What was startling was that many of these therapists were reporting that clients were also physically ill, with auto-immune problems, thyroid problems, multiple sclerosis, and other muscle and connective tissue diseases as well as mysterious ailments for which a diagnosis cannot be found. Plus somatization disorder is commonly found in these clients. Many of the clients who have been involved in human experimentation with the government, have multiple medically-documented physical ailments and I was really shocked today to hear one of the speakers talk about the cysts and the teeth breaking off because I have a client that that is happening to. Many of the people are afraid to tell their doctors their histories as mind control subjects for fear of being considered to be crazy. These clients have named same of the same people; particularly Dr. Greene, who was associated with client reports of childhood induction of pain, childhood mind control techniques, and childhood sexual abuse. One of my clients who had seen him with a name tag, identified him as Dr. L. Wilson Greene. A person with this same name was the Scientific Director of the Chemical and Radiological Laboratories at the Army Chemical Centre, and that he was engaged in doing research for the army and other intelligence agencies. Other names that have come to light are Dr. Sidney Gottlieb, Dr. Martin Orne (who it is reported were also involved in radiation research). It needs to be made clear that people have remembered these names and events spontaneously, with free recall, and without the use of any extraordinary retrieval techniques such as hypnosis. As much as possible, we have tried to verify the memories with family members, records, and experts in the field. Many attempts have been made through Freedom of Information filings to gain access to the mind control research documentation. Requests have generally been slowed down, or denied; although some information has been obtained. Which suggests that at least some of the information supplied by these clients is true. It is important that we obtain all of the information contained in CIA and military files to verify or deny our clients' memories. Although many of the files for MKULTRA may have been destroyed, whatever is left, along with the files for other projects, such as BLUEBIRD and ARTICHOKE to name only two, contain valuable information.

Furthermore, if, as the evidence suggests, some of these people were used in radiation experiments, there might be information in the mind control experiment files on radiation experiments. We need this information to help in the rehabilitation and treatment of many people who have severe psychological and medical problems which interfere with their social, emotional and financial well-being. Finally, I urge you to recommend an investigation into these matters. Although there was a Commission on Mind Control, it did not include experiments on children, because most of them were too young, or still involved in research in the late 1970's to come forward. The only way to end the harassment and suffering of these people is to make public what has happened to them in the mind control experiments. Please recommend that there be an investigation and that the files be opened on the mind control experiments as they related to children. Thank you.

Chris deNicola: Good afternoon. I am Chris deNicola, born July 1952, rendering me thirty-two years of age. I was a subject in radiation, as well as mind control and drug experiments performed by a man I knew as Dr. Greene. My parents were divorced around 1966 and Donald Richard Ebner, my natural father, was involved with Dr. Greene in the experiments. I was a subject in 1966 to 1976. Dr. Greene performed radiation experiments on me in 1970 focusing on my neck, throat and chest. 1972 focusing on my chest, and focusing on my uterus in 1975. Each time I became dizzy, nauseous and threw up. All these experiments were performed on me in conjunction with mind control techniques and drugs in Tucson, Arizona. Dr. Greene was using me mostly as a mind control subject from 1966 to 1973. His objective was to gain control of my mind and train me to be a spy assassin. The first significant memory took place at Kansas City University in 1966. Don Ebner took me there by plane when my mom was out of town. I was in what looked like a laboratory and there seemed to be other children. I was strapped down, naked, spread-eagled on a table on my back. Dr. Greene had electrodes on my body, including my head. He used what looked like an overhead projector and repeatedly said he was burning different images into my brain while a red light flashed aimed at my forehead. In between each sequence, he used electroshock on my body and told me to go deeper and deeper, deeper. While repeating each image, would go deeper into my brain and I would do whatever he told me to do. I felt drugged because he had given me a shot before he started the procedure. When it was over, he gave me another shot. The next thing I remember I was with my grandparents again in Tucson, Arizona. I was four years old.

You can see from this experiment that Dr. Greene used trauma, drugs, posthypnotic suggestion and more trauma in an effort to gain total control over my mind. He used me in radiation experiments both for the purposes of determining the effects of radiation on various parts of my body and to terrorize me as an additional trauma in the mind control experiments. The rest of the experiments took place in Tucson, Arizona out in the desert. I was taught how to pick locks, be secretive, use my photographic memory and a technique to withhold information by repeating numbers to myself. Dr. Greene moved on to wanting me to kill dolls that looked like real children. I stabbed a doll with a spear once after being severely traumatized, but the next time I refused. He used many pain induction techniques, but as I got older, I resisted more and more.

He often tied me down in a cage which was near his office. Between 1972 and 1976 he and his assistants were sometimes careless and left the cage unlocked. Whenever physically possible I snuck into his office and found files and memos addressed to CIA and military personnel. Included in these files were projects, sub-projects and experiment names with some code numbers about radiation and mind control experiments which I have submitted in the written documentation. I was caught twice and Dr. Green ruthlessly used electroshock, drugs, spun me on a table, put shocks on my stomach and my back, dislocated my joints, and used hypnotic techniques to make me feel crazy and suicidal.

Because of my rebellion and growing lack of cooperation, they gave up on me as a spy assassin. Consequently during the last two years, 1974-76, Dr. Greene used various mind control techniques to reverse the spy assassin messages, to self destruct and death messages. His purpose? He wanted me dead, and I struggled to stay alive all of my adult life. I believe it is by the grace of God that I am still alive. These horrible experiments have profoundly affected my life. I developed Multiple Personality Disorder because Dr. Greene's goal was to split my mind into as many parts as possible so he could control me totally. He failed, but I have to endure years of constant physical, mental and emotional pain even to this day. I have been in therapy consistently for twelve years, and it wasn't until I found my current therapist two and a half years ago, who had knowledge of the mind control experiments, that I have finally been able to make real progress and begin to heal.

In closing, I ask that you keep in mind that the memories I describe are but a glimpse of the countless others that took place in the ten years in between 1966 and 1976. That they weren't just radiation, but mind control and drug experiments as well. I have included more detailed information of what I remember in your written documentation. Please help us by recommending an investigation and making the information available so that therapists and other mental health professionals can help more people like myself. I know I can get better. I am getting better. And I know others can too. With the proper help. Please help us in an effort to prevent these heinous acts from continuing in the future. Thank you very much.

Claudia Mullen: Good afternoon. Between the years 1957 and 1984 I became a pawn in the government's game. Its ultimate goal was mind control and to create the perfect spy, all through the use of chemicals, radiation, drugs, hypnosis, electric shock, isolation in tubs of water, sleep deprivation, brainwashing, verbal, physical, emotional and sexual abuse. I was exploited unwittingly for nearly three decades of my life and the only explanations given to me were "that the end justifies the means" and "I was serving my country in their bold effort to fight communism". I can only summarize my circumstances by saying they took an already abused seven year old child and compounded my suffering beyond belief. The saddest part is, I know for a fact I was not alone. There were countless other children in my same situation and there was no one to help us until now. I have already submitted as much information as possible including conversations overheard at the agencies responsible. I am able to report all of this to you in such detail because of my photographic memory and the arrogance of the people involved. They were certain they would always control my mind. Although the process of recalling these atrocities is not an easy one, nor is it without some danger to myself and my family, I feel the risk is worth taking.

Dr. L. Wilson Greene received $50 million dollars from the Edgewood Chemical and Radiology Laboratory as part of the TSD, or Technical Science Division of the CIA, once described to Dr. Charles Brown that "children were used as subjects because they were more fun to work with and cheaper too. They needed lower profile subjects than soldiers and government people so only young willing females would do. Besides," he said, "I like scaring them. They in the Agency think I am a God, creating subjects in experiments for whatever deviant purposes Sid and James could think up" (Sid being Dr. Sidney Gottlieb; James is Dr. James Hamilton).

In 1958 they told me I was to be tested by some important doctors from the Society, or the Human Ecology Society and I was instructed to cooperate. I was told not to look at anyone's faces, and to try hard to ignore any names because this was a very secret project. I was told all these things to help me forget. Naturally, as most children do, I did the opposite and remembered as much as I could. A Dr. John Gittinger tested me, Dr. Cameron gave me the shock, and Dr. Greene the x-rays. Then I was told by Sid Gottliebe that "I was ripe for the big A" meaning ARTICHOKE. By the time I left to go home, just like every time from then on, I would remember only whatever explanations Dr. Robert G. Heath, of Tulane Medical University, gave me for the odd bruises, needle marks, burns on my head, fingers, and even the genital soreness. I had no reason to think otherwise. They had already begun to control my mind.

The next year I was sent to a lodge in Maryland called Deep Creek Cabins to learn how to sexually please men. I was taught how to coerce them into talking about themselves. It was Richard Helms, who was Deputy Director of the CIA, Dr. Gottlieb, Capt. George White, Morris Allan who all planned on filling as many high government agency officials and heads of academic institutions and foundations as possible so that later when the funding for mind control and radiation started to dwindle, projects would continue. I was used to entrap many unwitting men including themselves, all with the use of a hidden camera. I was only nine years old when the sexual humiliation began. I overheard conversations about part of the Agency called ORD which I found out was Office of Research and Development. It was run by Dr. Greene, Dr. Steven Aldrich, Martin Orne and Morris Allan. Once a crude remark was made by Dr. Gottlieb about a certain possible leak in New Orelans involving a large group of retarded children who had been given massive doses of radiation. He asked why was Wilson so worried about a few retarded kids, after all they would be the least likely to spill the beans.

Another time I heard Dr. Martin Orne, who was the director then of the Scientific Office and later head of the Institute for Experimental Research state that "in order to keep more funding coming from different sources for radiation and mind control projects", he suggested stepping up the amounts of stressors used and also the blackmail portions of the experiments. He said, "it needed to be done faster then to get rid of the subjects or they were asking for us to come back later and haunt them with our remembrances."

There is much more I could tell you about government sponsored research including project names, sub project numbers, people involved, facilities used, tests, and other forms of pain induction, but I think I have given more than enough information to recommend further investigation of all the mind control projects, especially as they involved so much of the use of the radiation.

I would love nothing more than to say that I dreamed this all up and need to just forget it. But that would be a tragic mistake. It would also be lie. All these atrocities did occur to me and to countless other children, and all under the guise of defending our country. It is because of the cumulative effects of exposure to radiation, chemicals, drugs, pain, subsequent mental and physical distress that I have been robbed of the ability to work and even to bear children of my own. It is blatantly obvious that none of this was needed, nor should ever have been allowed to take place at all, and the only means we have to seek out the awful truth and bring it to light is by opening whatever files remain on all the projects, and through another Presidential Commission on Mind Control.

I believe that every citizen of this nation has the right to know what is fact, and what is fiction. It is our greatest protection against this ever happening again. In conclusion, I can offer you no more than what I have given you today -- the truth. And I thank you for your time.

Testimony: Questions

Committee Spokesperson: Thank you for your presentations. We appreciate that this is not an easy thing to do. Are there comments or questions?

Dr. Duncan C. Thomas, Professor, University of Southern California, School of Medicine, Department of Preventive Medicine, Los Angeles, California: Can I ask either of you where were your parents through all this? Do you have any idea how you were recruited in the first place? Did you have parents? Did your parents know anything about what was going on?

Chris DeNicola: I can make a brief statement on that. It was my father who was involved with Dr. Greene. My mother was not aware because they were divorced when I was four years old, before that ... separated. What would happen, how he gained access to me is that these experiments actually took place in the middle of the night, and he would sneak in while my Mom was asleep, take me out and she had absolutely no knowledge of what happened. However, when these memories did surface, and I began to tell her about them, there was no question in her mind that he was capable. He had been in the military, in the Air Force. He had access to meet Dr. Greene, so in answer to your question, it was my father. He groomed me from the very beginning, started sexually abusing me from the very beginning, and it was just something that he wanted to do and he was closely involved with Dr. Greene, but my Mom had no knowledge. The only thing she knew was that she wanted to get away from him. She didn't know why. She just knew she had to get away from him because of my reaction to him. I am sorry, I didn't mean to go on. Thank you.

Claudia Mullen: Do you want an answer from me also?

Dr. Thomas: That's up to you.

Claudia Mullen: The way I got involved was I was adopted when I was two and a half years old by a woman who sexually abused me, and then she was a friend of the Chairman of the Board of Tulane University at the time. As a favour ... I began to exhibit symptoms of typical childhood abuse beginning very young and she asked him to recommend a child psychiatrist and it was Dr. Heath who was involved .... dissociate and that I had almost perfect recall and I passed all the personality tests that they gave me. Heath suggested me for the project. That's how I got into it. My father had no idea. He died when I was very young, but I don't know if my mother knew or not. I don't think she really cared to tell you the truth. Then she died when I was a teenager so ... after that they had access to me from then on.

Lois L. Norris, Second Vice President of Omaha National Bank and Omaha National Corporation (Retired), Omaha, Nebraska: You mentioned that there are others across the country who are recalling similar things. Do they all cover the same time span, generally, or do you have a feel for that?

Valerie Wolf: Generally they cover the same time span from about the late 1940's until ... one of the things that we are hearing about is that people were assigned to monitor them in case they should start to remember because it is so horrible what was done ... so we are not exactly sure when the actual experimentation took place and when it got into just the monitoring to make sure they were still under control and not everybody is being monitored. Pretty much from the late 1940's through the 1970's ... and maybe even into 1984 …

Claudia Mullen: Later than that I found out. Because after my parents died, there was no one to protect me ... my particular monitor was a physician at Tulane University and so he was a family friend also and he just kept on making sure that I kept going back and forgetting.

Valerie Wolf: So it's kind of unclear as to when or whether it stopped, or where ...

Claudia Mullen: They still monitor you though. I am in some danger coming here today because I am still being watched.

Valerie Wolf: I know it sounds unbelievable but there is actual ... she gets stuff in the mail, she gets phone calls, people are writing things on her house, using the pseudonym that they used when she was at Tulane and only they would know that name.

Claudia Mullen: My real name was never used. Never.

Lois L. Norris: Were they all children at the time?

Valerie Wolf: Yes. All children. And the thing is, as therapists, we are trying really hard to figure this out and to get as much information as we can. Claudia's memories have been verified ... a lot of them. The way I have approached this is, I don't read in the field. So as people give me information, I send them to experts like Alan Scheflin who has a lot of information, and then he will get back to me to confirm or deny. He has never denied any information that I have sent him. Some of it can't be because we don't have all the information, but a lot of Claudia's memories have been validated, and they are not in any published source. The only way she would know the things she knows is if she had filed for Freedom of Information Act information. This is what Alan Scheflin is telling me. I have been very careful not to know a whole lot, so if someone tells me something, I don't even cue them because I don't know either.

Dr. Duncan Thomas: It seems to me that documentary evidence is going to be key to establishing the truth of these claims. It is hard for me to imagine that a program as large and as complex as you people have described, could have gone on for so long without a great deal of documentation. The question is, where is this documentation now? It becomes a Catch-22. If it is said that all the documentation resides within the CIA files, then all of it is secret and they won't give it to us, but what you have described is a pattern of a very complex organization which involves plenty of people outside of the CIA as well. Therefore there must be a substantial amount of documentation that could be discovered. You just mentioned the letters that some of you are still receiving. There is a lead to documentation. Can you describe to me what efforts have been made, either by yourselves or by other people who are working on this story to track down some of this documentation? And what you meant a moment ago when you said that similar memories have been verified or validated …

Valerie Wolf: Dr. Alan Scheflin, you have his resume in the documentation and a statement from him about Claudia, he has been for the past twenty years filing Freedom of Information Act filings to get this information ... has been piecing it together. Other people across the country have been doing the same, going back to the government files, getting what they can. And what they have also been doing is writing books, sharing information. So he has actual Freedom of Information Act information. The problem is when the requests are going in now, they are being slowed down, or denied, just kind of lost in the shuffle -- and the information is very difficult to get.

Dr. Duncan Thomas: I am sorry. I don't see the documentation in the package provided to me. Is there something missing.

Valerie Wolf: I sent a packet of documentation overnight mail ... it should have been here on Monday, and more yesterday.

Hearting Spokeperson: If we haven't received it, we will let you know.

Valerie Wolf: I sent the first one to Steve Claydman and the second one to Kristin Crotti (?). Again, it was what I could pull together in about a week and a half from across the country ... it is the consistency of the stories. The thing is we want to verify, so

Alan has amassed over 20 years from Freedom of Information Act, from memos other people give him, or sharing information ... a lot of information. But we don't have the complete story. There is still a lot of stuff that we don't know, and that's what we are trying to find out because …

Dr. Duncan Thomas: Does any of this documentation specifically refer to radiation experiments? Because we are told by CIA that they never did any radiation experiments. What we need is documentation in order to pursue that.

Claudia Mullen: All you have to do is look up everything on ORD (Office of Research and Development) the one I overheard them speaking about. That was almost strictly radiation. And that was run by Dr. Steven Aldrich, Martin Orne …

Dr. Duncan Thomas: And that's included in the package you sent Steven Claydman.

Claudia Mullen: Yes. I gave him project numbers, project names, sub-project numbers ... even the subjects ... we were given numbers ourselves for each specific experiment and I overheard my number because they assumed ... they used techniques so you would forget. When you go home, you wouldn't remember what happened. So they just talked freely ... that's why no one ever hid their face, wore a mask or anything because they knew that I would not remember. And I didn't. I did not remember until two years ago.

Valerie Wolf: I think you could also follow up on Dr. L. Wilson Greene. I don't know if you have come across him, but he seems to have been involved in both. And I think, realistically in terms of the mind control, some of the subjects were used in mind control and radiation, some as you have been hearing have been strictly radiation, and some were strictly mind control. I think the reason it is coming up now is because in some of the stuff people are remembering, they knew that it would break down. They really worked hard to induce amnesia, and they knew it would break down, and I think in the last couple of years that is what has been happening because we have been hearing more and more and ... so we are just trying to find out what's happening here. So we would appreciate any help you could give us.

Chris Ebner: I just wanted to address you (Dr. Duncan Thomas) for a moment ... the question you asked about the documentation on radiation specifically ... included in my packet and I don't know if you have that or not. It's entitled "Radiation File Information". There are subject names, experiment names, and some code numbers that I remembered. The problem is that we have no way of verifying that without opening the files.

Address by Her Majesty Queen Silvia of Sweden at the Round Table of Business community against the Trafficking of Human Beings

Athens, January 23, 2006

Your Majesty

Your Excellencies

Ladies and Gentlemen

In August of 1996 the first World Congress against Commercial Sexual Exploitation of Children was organised in Stockholm. Representatives of 122 governments, many non-governmental organisations, law enforcement, the travel industry and others were gathered and I was asked to be the Patron of this first World Congress. I have ever since actively followed the actions to combat the problem, taken by governments, NGOs and the corporate sector.

Having been made aware of the devastating consequences for the children, the most innocent and vulnerable of all victims, I took the initiative to establish in 1999 World Childhood Foundation. Childhood is fortunate to work directly with the corporate world. This co-operation is beneficial for us both. For us, of course, their financial support and their advice are the most important. For the companies it means taking social responsibility, which creates a lot of good-will in the community at large and - not the least essential - among their employees. They feel proud and happy to work in a company, which takes social responsibility and I think we all know that more and more companies are realizing the importance of being regarded as 'a good citizen'. Today we have 14 co-founders and three Major Partners.

An important field for Childhood is to support initiatives in the combat against sexual abuse of children as well as to provide treatment and support to these children. Presently World Childhood Foundation is supporting 76 projects in 14 countries.

It was also based on the World Congress that the 'Code of Conduct for the Protection of Children from Sexual Exploitation in Travel and Tourism' was developed in 1998 by ECPAT Sweden and adopted by the main part of the Swedish travel industry. The Code is currently implemented globally. 68 travel companies from 18 countries and 3 major international hotel chains are signatories of the Code of Conduct. The number of tourists impacted by the Code is estimated to over 30 million per year. Concrete examples of the implementation are training of the staff of the travel industry as well providing information to travellers through websites, brochures, catalogues or in-flight videos onboard the plane. Travellers are made aware of how children are being sexually exploited for profit and what they can do to prevent it.

Enlisting the support of the Swedish corporate sector I am proud to inform you that all major Swedish Internet service providers, since last year, are blocking access to the commercial child pornographic web sites. According to National Police statistics 20-30.000 attempts per day to access commercial child pornographic web sites are now stopped in Sweden.

Also, according to National Police, the majority of victims of trafficking are brought to Sweden via the ferries operating on the Baltic Sea. I am very pleased that one of these major ferry companies, which also is one of Childhood's co-founders, is now taking preventive measures against trafficking; their staff has been trained and written material on trafficking in several languages is available onboard.

I much appreciate that all of you have been given the opportunity here in Athens to see the film Lilya 4-ever. Identifying the Swedish corporate sector's contribution to combating the trafficking of human beings, I would like to place the production company of Lilya 4-ever, *Memphis Film* and the director Mr Lukas Moodysson, on top of that list. They have made it possible to raise the awareness of millions of individuals, not only in Sweden, but in no less than 56 other countries on all continents to which the film was distributed commercially. The film is also frequently used for educational purposes by schools, police academies, judges and prosecutors, non-governmental organizations and other institutions in several countries. It has furthermore been screened in the Parliaments of Sweden, Russia, Belgium and other countries and is a compulsory part of the training for all Swedish peace keeping troops to the Balkans and other destinations. Lilya 4-ever was also nominated for an Oscar award.

The film Lilya 4-ever manifests not only the extreme vulnerability of the victims but also the importance the demand factor has for maintaining this lucrative business in human bodies. Very sadly, the film is based on a real case of trafficking to Sweden:

Her name was Dangoule. She was a 16 year old girl from Lithuania with the same dreams and the same hopes for the future as any other teenager. She was enticed by the man she loved and trusted to go to Sweden with promises of a better life and a steady job picking vegetables. She arrived to Kristianstad, a city in the south of Sweden, on the 17 th of November 1999. Her passport was taken from her and she was locked up in an apartment and told that she now had a debt of 20.000 Euros for her travel, passport and accommodation costs. Dangoule was beaten, raped, starved and humiliated. Her pimp told her that if she informed anyone of her situation, she would be thrown in prison since prostitution is a crime in Sweden. Moreover, she was an illegal immigrant since her passport was faked. The terror forced Dangoule to be silent and to suffer several customers per day. On the 7 th of January 2000, in utter despair, Dangoule jumped from a bridge to end her life.

In one of the last sequences of the film you saw Lilya being taken away by the ambulance. In real life 16 year old Dangoule survived another few days in hospital. She however never regained consciousness and died alone and deprived of all dignity in a foreign country. Her identity and other circumstances would have remained unknown for always, had not police found a piece of paper with a telephone number in her clothes. The telephone number led police to the apartment where she had been kept prisoner. Dangoule´s few belongings were found, including some letters she had written to friends in Lithuania. These letters made police eventually identify her friends, who could fill in the missing parts of Dangoule´s short life in her home country. The trafficker was never identified. In a last attempt to pursue the legal case, the police made an announcement on Swedish TV requesting information from the public. Surprisingly, a man came forward. He was Russian by nationality and admitted that he had been paid to take Dangoule from the airport to the apartment upon her arrival to Sweden. He claimed that he did not realize that this was a case of trafficking and that he had no further information. Due to lack of legislation at the time, specifically targeting trafficking of human beings, the man was set free. In fact, no one was prosecuted for the trafficking of Dangoule; for assaulting her, deceiving her, buying her body, raping her or causing her tragic death.

Had this case taken place two and a half years later, after 1 st of July 2002, when a comprehensive law was introduced in Sweden, targeting all phases of trafficking of human beings, that is, the recruitment, transport, providing accommodation, the advertising and the selling of sexual services, the Russian man would have been prosecuted and convicted.

But let us take a step further back in time: Had Dangoule had a higher level of education, would she not have realized that picking vegetables was not a realistic job offer in the middle of the Scandinavian winter? Had the passport officer in the airport had special training on trafficking of human beings, would she not have inspected Dangoule´s passport more carefully, maybe to detect that it was faked? Had the general public had more knowledge of trafficking, would not someone in the building where she was locked up have reacted to Dangoule´s screaming and the coming and going of different men? To these rhetoric questions I believe we find some important answers how to combat trafficking. Finally, had not Dangoule´s traffickers correctly counted on the demand factor, would Sweden have represented a lucrative market? Trafficking of human beings functions like any commercial business: with no demand there is no supply.

I am very pleased that the corporate sector has become such

an important ally and that they are represented here in substantial numbers. There is no doubt that large corporations or small businesses have important contributions to make. And there is no doubt that the industry benefits from taking strong action against trafficking.

In my address here today I have focused on trafficking of minors for sexual purposes. I am aware that considerable trafficking is taking place also for other purposes, such as labour, begging, delinquency and adoption. Also that boys, as young as five, are trafficked to be used as camel jockeys. According to the International Organization for Migration, IOM, some 90% of the global trafficking is for sexual purposes and some 50% of the victims are minors, using the definition of the United Nations Convention on the Rights of the Child, that is up to 18 years.

In conclusion I would like to share with you the following:

To see but not to see,
to see but to deny,
to see but not to act,
is a crime against a child!
You can make a difference!
You can stop this slavery!
You can save a child!

Stop the collaboration with non ethical hotels and do not tolerate those that promote or accept sexual services with minors.

Be a responsible company, a clean company, by guaranteeing your employees and your clients that there is no access possible on your company computers to child pornography.

Do inform your employees to be alert, do cooperate with the police and never erase this illegal material if it ever is downloaded.

Every pimp and every perpetrator should know: also you are watching them!

Thank you for being here, thank you to care: you can make a difference!

A warm thank you to our hosts who have taken this extremely valuable initiative and have organized this excellent and successful meeting to End Human Trafficking Now!

Postscript:
Satanic Apologetics

By Tracy R. Twyman

There is a branch of Christian theological studies called "apologetics." Basically, this is the science of providing refutations (or attempted refutations) of criticisms against the orthodox interpretation of Christian scripture. As the name "apologetics" implies, this often involves back-peddling, equivocating, and squirming out of hard questions, providing excuses and otherwise "apologizing" for the inexplicable nature of their beliefs, and the utter failure of their logic. It is sad, pathetic, and embarrassing to witness argument between a Christian apologetic and a religious skeptic: you are embarrassed for the Christian, whose arguments are so weak, and you are embarrassed for the skeptic, who takes such childish glee in shooting down the false premises of a mental midget.

Unfortunately, many people whose religious interests could be classified as "occult" feel the need to resort to "apologetics" when confronted by an orthodox Christian with the "Satanic" nature of their beliefs. They claim that there is nothing "Satanic" or "Luciferian" about their interests, and that the Christians are simply "misinterpreting" an ancient tradition that predates the concepts of both Christ and the Devil. Some even claim to be more truly "Christian" than their detractors, throwing around New Age terms like "Christ-consciousness."

In my opinion, this is hair-splitting. I suppose one has the right not to call oneself a "Satanist" or a "Luciferian" overtly. But the fact is that there is a Luciferian aspect to every occult belief or science. All Hermetic arts ultimately descend from the ancient race of gods represented as fallen angels in the Bible and *The Book of Enoch*. Therefore the occult is inherently Satanic. Indeed, many Judeo-Christian traditions also carry a Luciferian heritage. Some even believe that Christ himself was a descendant of the Watchers, and practiced magical rites that were Luciferian in nature. The same is believed regarding Christ's ancestors, King

David and King Solomon, while even earlier ancestors such as Adam, Noah, Abraham, Isaac, and Jacob, are said to be figures representing these ancient Luciferian god-kings. This would mean that Judeo-Christianity is inherently Luciferian. So why, then, should an occultist be ashamed to admit that his traditions are Luciferian in nature?

The worst perpetrators of "Satanic apologetics" are those who openly call themselves "Satanists", especially members of the Church of Satan. These people claim to speak for the Satanic tradition, and yet they relegate Satan to the position of being an "archetype", with no real existence, historical or otherwise. To them, Satan merely represents "intellectual rebellion." Some even argue a semantic difference between the terms "Satan", "Lucifer", and "the Devil." Their beliefs are, at bottom, atheistic, and if they worship anyone, it is themselves.

What is really annoying is how Church of Satan members assume that all other followers of Satanic traditions are like they are. Thus the practice of Satanic apologetics spreads to "debunking" of phenomena like Satanic human sacrifice, Satanic Ritual Abuse, and Satanic conspiracy theories. Recently, a Church of Satan representative was on Linda Vester's "Dayside" show on Fox News debunking the notion that Laci Peterson could have been killed by Satanists. Real Satanists, she argued, are abstract philosophers, embracing a system of self-empowerment. Real Satanists have no desire to kill anybody. Real Satanists don't even actually worship Satan. This woman could not conceive that a group of people who call themselves Satanists, or that are perceived as Satanists by outsiders, might exist that do not share her abstract notions about the "Satan archetype." She could not conceive that such a group might exist which perpetuated the ancient religious traditions of our ancestors: traditions that certainly at one time included both human and animal sacrifice, and which would most certainly be perceived as "Satanic" today. People like her believe that Satanism, instead of stretching back to antiquity, was begun out of a vacuum in 1966 by Anton LaVey in Southern California. Such a claim, of course, flies in the face of the numerous cases of murders that have been committed by people who later admitted to being motivated by Satanism. While such cases are not epidemic, they certainly do take place. There are also hundreds of murders that take place in Africa every year as sacrifices to traditional African gods. Similar animistic religions prevail throughout the Third World, and in many cases have spread to the First World as well. And while the number of human sacrifices that take place in the First World is undoubtedly limited, the number of animal sacrifices made in the name of Voudon and Santeria is too high to be counted. While the participants might not label themselves Satanists, they are certainly worshipping demonic beings, and their practices are perceived as such by outsiders.

But Satanic apologists will still tell you that nothing like this ever takes place. I have heard similar arguments about Satanic Ritual Abuse. While it is true that many of the alleged "victims" of SRA who have gone public have since been proven to be lying, delusional or both, to say that such a thing "never happens" is to ignore the endless amounts of bizarre behavior that human beings indulge in. Furthermore, it is no real secret that "Sex-magic" rites, including the practice of sexual aberrations, have been at the core of occult sciences from the very beginning. The rites of the priests of Babylon, Egypt, Greece, Rome, and India all involved sex rituals, with temple prostitution as an integral part of their tradition, as have the priesthoods of numerous other cultures. Judaism, and later Christianity, were really part of a small minority of religious traditions that did not include, overtly at least, the practices of human sacrifice and sacred sex. Throughout the Old Testament, the priests of Israel are shown struggling desperately to keep the public, the monarchy, and even their fellow priests, pure of the religious taint of the heathen gods of their neighbors – an insurmountable task when confronted with a perpetual onslaught of overwhelmingly persuasive influence. This was the case especially whenever the sons of Israel made wives or concubines of the women of heathen nations. Wise King Solomon is famous for having dabbled in the magical arts and the worship of "false gods." But he is equally well-known for his exceptionally large harem of foreign women. It perhaps goes without saying that the sex practices of these ancient cults rarely stayed within the bounds considered acceptable by modern standards. Homosexuality, bestiality, and group orgies were common, and there was certainly no age restriction on the participants, nor any requirement at all that the participants be consenting. Rape was common, and the murder of the victim before, during, or after the sex rite was common as well. Infanticide or abortion was not an uncommon end for the unhappy fruits of these unions. In other instances, the children were raised with privileges, as the divine offspring of the god to whom the ceremony had been dedicated.

Indeed, the tradition of sex magic began with such a mating between gods and humans. I speak, of course, about the interbreeding between the "sons of God" and the "wives of men" that is written of in *Genesis 6*. This incident is elaborated on greatly in *The Book of Enoch*, and other apocryphal texts, where these "sons of God" are also referred to as "the Watchers", and are described as fallen angels. *The Book of Enoch* portrays the Watchers as being consumed with lust upon the sight of human women, and as they descended from Heaven, "their parts of shame hung down like horses."

According to a website called "multiorgasmic.com", the Watchers, or "Nephilim" as they're called in the Bible, were of a much higher level of sexual potency than human males, capable of having limitless orgasms without the "Male Refractory Period" (MRP) that prevents most men from doing this. The website claims that the Watchers taught human females how to enjoy multiple orgasms as well. *The Book of Enoch* and other texts seem to back up this assertion. The Watchers were accused by God of Teaching women sexual abominations they had never before known, and of teaching them the use of make-up and jewelry, by which means they went about seducing human males. Thus was rampant promiscuity and fornication spread about the land, forcing God to bring about the Flood, to wipe the Earth clean of this pestilence.

The children born of these unions between angels and human women were described variously as "giants" in some instances, and in others identified by the word "Rephaim." Multiorgasmic.com claims that this terms comes from the root word "Rapha", which they translate to mean "hard, potent, masculine, male, or virile." This links up with a Canaanite legend regarding a line of fallen kings known as "rp'um" – "Dispersers of Fertility." This links up with the legend of the Cainites (the descendants of Cain), who were said to have been so sexually insatiable that they kept two separate sets of wives: one for the purposes of procreation, and the other for the purposes of pleasure.

But there is evidence indicating that it was not only heterosexual unions that the Watchers and their sons were interested in. When in *Genesis* the two Watchers visit Lot in the land of Sodom, the local inhabitants become consumed with lust, and besiege Lot's house, demanding to be allowed to sodomize the angels. Something about their very appearance inspired this desire in the Sodomites. A similar scene occurs when in *The Book of Judges*, a young Levite goes to visit a friend in the land of the Benjamites (descendants, according to multiorgasmic.com, of the Rephaim). A group of Benjamites called the "sons of Belial" again besiege the house, demanding homosexual intercourse with the Levite. Clearly, the Watchers and their descendants are associated with promiscuity of every sort, which was brought into the world by them in the first place. This tradition of perversion, therefore, originated with Satan, and was passed on through the generations to his progeny.

Multiorgasmic.com claims that descendants of this race can be found today, and that they possess virility and sexual capacity beyond that of normal human males. Indeed, various records stretching from Biblical times to modern times give us every reason to believe that the bloodline of the fallen angels has continued, and that their traditions, including their sexual practices, have been passed down as well. This "tradition" includes the hermetic sciences and ritual magic, including, most especially, sexual magic. Thus, the sex mysteries can be found embedded within the rites of witchcraft, Satanism, Gnosticism, and secret orders such as the Knights Templar, the Rosicrucians, the Ordo Templi Orientis, the Dragon Order, and many others too numerous to be named. Sexual symbolism is at the heart of every religious mythology, and even where the rites are no longer practiced (such as in Orthodox Christianity, Judaism, and Islam), the metaphors remain. The idea of sex magic begins with a simple concept: that the union between a man and a woman can, through spiritual practices, be used to mimic intercourse with divine beings. But sex magic includes within its repertoire every sexual act imaginable. Homosexuality, bestiality, pedophilia, sado-masochism, and the like all have their value within the rites of sex magic, as practiced by various groups throughout the centuries.

Those who use Satanic apologetics against Satanic conspiracy theories are by far the worst. To be fair, most of the personal testimonials floating around today by those who have supposedly seen in action the "Satanic Illuminati that controls the world" are indeed false. But the overall notion of the conspiracy cannot be. It is true that a large number of powerful people in the world, both today and throughout history, have been members of occult secret societies, practicing the Luciferian traditions that ultimately came from Cain. An overwhelming number of these people are from royal bloodlines that also ultimately derive from Cain. In other words, they are Luciferians. And the groups that these people belong to do appear to embrace a long-term plan, not only for world-domination, but for the restructuring of the world's institutions along the lines of their own religious ideals - ideals that are, at bottom, Luciferian. And it would be hard for me to say that the world which they appear to be making does not resemble shockingly the biblical description of the Antichrist's kingdom. It does *indeed* resemble that. But it also resembles in many ways the prophesized kingdom of god which is to follow. Therein lies the beauty of the grand plan of the initiates who occupy society's upper strata. Their beliefs involve a mingling of powers both infernal and divine, and they want to create a New World Order that reflects both.

In summation, for Satanists to say that there is no real "Satan" in Satanism is to deny the truly evocative power that Satan (or Lucifer) possesses. Furthermore, for occultists to claim that there is nothing "Satanic" about what they are doing demonstrates their ignorance of the true origin of the occult tradition. When we deny Satan, we deny God as well, and render our creeds hollow, our beliefs meaningless. To me, if Satanists are *not* committing sacrifices, indoctrinating the young, and trying to control the world, and if occultism has nothing to do with Satan, then what is the point? Why should anyone be interested? What sets these people apart from those snotty, pretentious asses who sit behind us in philosophy class, splitting apart semantics and droning in their smug, nasally voices about "subjectivity" and "abstraction"? If you have to deny the power of Satan in order to feel comfortable with your chosen religious beliefs, then perhaps you should consider being an atheist. Satanists and occultists who deny Satan whose those alternative belief systems simply because they were bored with religion. And as my step-father used to say, "If you're bored, you're boring." There is nothing more boring than a pathetic Satanic apologist. I'll take a paranoid Christian fanatic over one of those any day of the week.

The Biological Basis of Elitism and "Divine Right" Rule

By Tracy R. Twyman

On October 28th, 1998, a number of newspapers across the country ran an Associated Press article entitled "Presidential Hopefuls Share Blue Blood Lines." The article, based on information put forth by Burke's Peerage, claimed that every single President of the United States has had a notable amount of royal European ancestry, and in each Presidential race, the one with the most royal genes is the one who wins - every single time. This tendency has been noted in supposedly Democratic European politics as well, prompting some to charge that a global conspiracy exists to keep power within the hands of a specific gene pool. This charge is not entirely baseless, and many books have been written tracing modern aristocratic bloodlines back to the royal houses of Israel, Egypt, Sumer, and beyond. The charge is further supported by the fact that many of the supposed conspirators proudly boast about the ancient origins of their ancestry. The traditional explanation for why power is passed down through the ages by blood has been the mystical Divine Right of Kings. This dates back to the 17th century and states that a king is created by God, so therefore kingly authority resides in the blood irrespective of anything else. Many have claimed that there is a genetic characteristic carried in the blood itself which makes this so. But what would it be? Is there a legitimate physiological reason behind the Divine Right of Kings?

Fields of the Nephilim

The all-important element of the Divine Right is that it comes from God, or "the gods", alternately. And who were these gods? Authors such as Zecharia Sitchin, Sir Laurence Gardner and Nicholas de Vere are authoritatively convinced that kingship was created by an advanced race of beings called the Annunaki, also called the Nephilim in the Old Testament. These were the ones who created the human race and interbred with a portion of it to create the kingly caste which until this day has still maintained control over the Earth. These celestial creatures have been variously identified with Dragons, Elves, Fairies, Gnomes, Leprechauns, Sprites, Nymphs, Pixies, Angels, Demons, Devils, Witches, Giants, Vampires, Werewolves, and just about every mythical being you can imagine. Some, like Gardner and Sitchin, claim that they come from another planet. Others, like de Vere, say that they're multi-dimensional, or that they're from the Hollow Earth. Some, like David Icke, say that they are humans inhabited by the spirits of multidimensional reptiles, capable of shapeshifting into reptile form at any time. Still others claim that they were humanoid, but more than human, with pale white skin. The human hybrid offspring that they created as the royal/priestly caste was, according to most, the Aryans, who usually had red hair with green eyes - in stark contrast to the traditional Hitlerian vision. Nicholas de Vere, the leader of an organization called The Dragon Court which claims to represent this royal Aryan caste, writes, "the depiction of the Aryan (Scythian) as a tall, ruddy-complexioned blonde racist yeoman-farmer-warrior-god has no basis in truth." He further suggests that the "yeoman-farmer" Celtic, Gaulish and Pictish tribes which we now think of as Aryan were actually of a different race, but had hired the extra-human Aryans to be their leaders. These Aryans were also the masterminds behind the Indian, Hittite, Greek, Egyptian, Hebrew, Sumerian and Pre-Sumerian Ubaid civilizations. Many believe that their descendants can be found amongst the segment of the population with the RH Negative blood type, roughly 5% of the Earth's population, most of them Europeans. These people are often born with an extra vertebrate, have a lower than normal body temperature, and can rarely mate with one another successfully, suggesting that they may indeed be a hybrid species. Conspiracy enthusiast Arizona Wilder takes it a step further by saying, "The Aryan bloodline is alien to this planet... There are 13 bloodlines from this kind of stock (the Merovingians being one), and all of them have to a greater or lesser degree the capacity to play host to the Shape Changer reptiles." The other 12 families have been identified as Astor, Bundy, Collins, Dupont, Freeman, Kennedy, Li, Onassis, Reynolds, Rockefeller, Rothschild, Russell, and Van Duyn, with the rest of the European royal families being categorized as "Merovingian." These are the people referred to by the fanatic group the Sons of Jared when they "pledge an implacable war against the descendants of the Watchers, who as notorious pharaohs, kings and dictators, have throughout history dominated mankind... like super-gangsters, a celestial Mafia ruling the world." The Book of Enoch says that the sons of the Nefilim are destined to "afflict, oppress, destroy, attack, do battle and work destruction on the earth."

Nicholas de Vere, himself a Prince of the Dragon Blood, sees it quite differently. He sees them as the rightful shepherds of the human flock. "The fairies were tuned to a higher frequency of perception and activity generally. In the past, therefore, because the Fairies were, for millennia, physiologically bred and exhaustively trained to operate at a higher level than men, humans often invited the to become social navigators... A dragon was one who saw clearly, and the clarity of vision engendered was always classically associated with wisdom, which itself produces power...." The Annunaki and their quasi-human offspring are attributed remarkable traits. They lived for thousands of years, were capable of levitation, dimension-hopping, clairvoyance, and a million other magical powers, all a product of applied eugenics. "Selective unions gave the race the opportunity to breed outstanding magicians whose gift of natural perception and understanding: and whose ability to access the 'Otherworld', helped to produce and guide brilliant kings who ruled with elegant aplomb. The ability to perform magic was carried in the blood", and "the Elves were relied upon by their client races to be able to see things and perform feats that these client races couldn't." Laurence Gardner, himself a former member of the Dragon Court, concurs. "In short, these people were bred to be leaders of mankind, and they were both mentally and physically maintained in the highward state." But what property did they inherit in the blood which makes this possible? The experts are nearly unanimous about the fact that the answer is endocrinology. Says de Vere, "hormonal levels [are] influenced by genetic inheritance and that hormones [affect] the individual's perceptions, psychological unicameralism and the subsequent ability to transcend and perceive the intricacies of the cosmos. Elven blood [is] rich in these substances."

Starfire Bloodfests

"The best blood is of the moon, monthly..."

Aleister Crowley, *The Book of the Law*

The beneficial effects of the hormone melatonin have been part of the health supplement scene for some time, for high melatonin production is known to be synonymous with a high immune system, a low cancer risk, long life, energy, stamina, and according to many, enhanced spiritual awareness. Perhaps it is fitting then that this hormone is secreted by the pineal gland, a mysterious little item long believed by mystics to be the "Seat of the Soul", "The Third Eye", and the organ through which psychic powers are exercised. In fact it actually functions as an organ of sight in some reptiles, and it still seems to possess some sensitivity to light in higher mammals, as melatonin production increases when the person is exposed to darkness (thus melatonin means "night worker.") Writes Laurence Gardner, "High melatonin production thereby increases the facility for receiving and transmitting high-frequency cosmic and local broadcasts, and leads to a greater state of cosmic awareness - a state simply of 'knowing.' In this regard, it is interesting to note that the Pineal Third Eye has been found to contain very fine granular particles, rather like the crystals in a wireless receiving set." Many magical rites and meditation techniques are aimed at gaining control of this organ and the fluid it produces, the live melatonin. Rumor has it that the members of the super-secret society Skull & Bones, which both George Bush and George Jr. belong to, engage in a ceremony called "The Obscene Rite", which involves the consumption of the live pineal gland of a human or animal sacrifice, in order to get the fresh secretions. Supplements bought over the counter are ineffective because, as Gardner explains, "their inherent secretions are obtained from the desiccated glands of dead animals and they lack the truly important elements which only exist in live human glandular manufacture."

But the Aryan overlords who ruled over mankind in ancient days had a simpler way of acquiring this fluid. Their ancestor-gods the Annunaki had endocrine systems that produced large amounts of this and other beneficial substances, so they drank it straight from the source: the menstrual blood and vaginal fluids of the goddesses themselves. This they referred to lovingly as "Starfire" and drank in a ritual ceremony called the Black Mass, after which the Catholic Mass is said to have been modeled. Later, as direct contact with the Annunaki ceased, the fluids were collected from sacred priestesses referred to as "Scarlet Women", or "Grail Maidens." Readers will recognize the Scarlet Woman as the Whore of Revelations, as well as the title which Aleister Crowley gave to all of his sex magick partners. "These sacred, royal princesses,", writes de Vere, "virgins of High Birth and Pure Blood, at an optimum age would be chosen to act as feeding females", whose essences contained such valuable substances as, "oxytocin, prolactin, melatonin, seratonin, adenosyne triphosphate, dopamine, telomerase, and retinol." There is another important ingredient in the mix here. De Vere explains, "many think that only men have semen, when in fact women also have it." And so a Starfire ritual involves the use of a golden straw. "Such a device would have been inserted into the virgin's urethra to the depth of about one inch, whilst the partner in the rite inserted his or her finger into the vagina and massaged the 'roof of the mouth' or uppermost wall of the cannel nearest the opening of the vagina, behind the public bone. After a few conducive moments perhaps, orgasm would occur and the fluid from the gland would discharge itself through the straw, either into the waiting mouth of the recipient, or onto a "grail platter' or dish held next to the vulva." Keen readers will recognize this as being identical to a sex magick ritual advocated by Aleister Crowley for members of his "Order or Oriental Templars" (OTO). The only difference is that his rite also involved the use of male semen which was called the "Red Tincture" or "coagulated blood", while the female fluids were called "Gluten" or "The White Tincture." Together they made "The Elixir of Life", and in sexual alchemy blood and semen are the primae materia or first matter of the great work. "This is the true Key to Magick", writes Crowley. "That is, by the right use of this secret man may impose his Will on Nature herself."

Monatomic Gold: The Substitute

But according to de Vere and others, ingesting the fluids of mundane women has only a slight effect, certainly not enough to maintain a royal Dragon family in the manner to which they're accustomed. And after a few thousand years the genetic purity of their Grail maidens began to deteriorate, so the Starfire lost its potency. This reportedly began around 1960 BC and is equated with the time that and edict was handed down to Noah by God demanding that the consumption of all blood cease immediately. (Gen. 9:4) Thus, a substitute had to be found, and so the alchemical process was created, as a means of artificially creating the Elixir of Life, the Philosopher's Stone, also known as "potable gold." This is created using a black powder known as occultum, the universal solvent which has the power to transmute metals. When placed against gold it converted it into a white powder which could be ingested. It is said to cause nothing less than immortality, as it sets off a self-correcting mechanism in your DNA that lasts for thousands of years. It also bestows the enhanced melatonin production and magical powers associated with Starfire, including clairvoyance, dimension-hopping and flying capabilities. It is believed that this "white gold" is the same as the "Shew-bread" and "Manna from Heaven" mentioned in the Old Testament.

Today, there are those who publicly proclaim knowledge of the Philosopher's Stone, and a man named David Hudson claims to have created a technique for manufacturing this white gold, which he's pattented as ORME (Orbitally Rearrangede Monatomic Elements.) Ormus is a name associated with the Holy Grail, and so readers may not be surprised to learn that Hudson himself is related to the Merovingian Grail family, through Claude de Guise. Basically, the powder is created by putting gold into a higher atomic state through a series of intense heating and cooling sessions, during which it loses and gains weight radically, as though portions of the mass were being transferred into another dimension. David Hudson continues about the magical quantum properties of his white gold:

> *"These M-state elements have been observed to exhibit superconductivity, superfluidity, Josephson tunneling and magnetic levitation... They may enhance energy flow in the microtubules inside every living cell. Ingesting m-state*

gold is different effects on the body than the effects of
ingesting metallic gold. At 2 mg. it totally has gotten rid of
Karposi Sarcomas on AIDS patients. Within 2 hours, their
white blood cell count goes from 2500 to 6500. ... Stage 4
cancer patients have taken it orally, and after 45 days have
no cancer left anyplace in the body. It's been used on Lou
Gehrig's disease, it's been used on MS, it's been used on
MD, it's been used on arthritis. It literally corrects the
DNA."

Sympathy for the Devil

All of this puts a nice, friendly face on the whole thing, a
secret power held only by an elite caste of Aryans who use it to
lord themselves over the rest of the human population. And there
are those who would say that the "substitute" white gold never did
away with the original practice of blood-drinking as a method for
obtaining the substances they needed. David Icke and his
associate, Arizona Wilder, have campaigned the globe to inform its
citizens with Chicken Little-like hysteria that most of its financiers,
politicians and aristocrats are actually under the control of
Reptilian beings from another dimension, who are inhabiting their
bodies. "To hold their human form, these entities need to drink
human (mammalian) blood and access the energy it contains to
maintain their DNA codes in their 'human' expression. If they
don't, they manifest their reptilian codes and we would all see what
they really look like." Icke believes that most of this blood is
obtained in human sacrifice rituals engaged in by the Satanic
Illuminati. "From what I understand from former 'insiders', the
blood (energy) of babies and small children is the most effective
for this, as are blond-haired, blue-eyed people. Hence these are the
ones overwhelmingly used in sacrifice, as are red- haired people
also." His compatriot, Arizona Wilder, goes into a bit more detail
when she writes, "They have a hypnotic gaze which fixes the
victim - in a trance of terror - which promotes secretion of the
pineal gland - at that point, they cannot hold human form any
longer and begin to shapeshift in anticipation of supper." Wilder,
claims to have witnessed Laurence Gardner drinking blood and
shapeshifting during a sacrifice at Montauk, New York, as well as

a number of others who were transformed during similar bloodfests, including, "Bush and his two sons, Albright, Kissinger, Reagan and Nancy, J. Rockefeller, Ford, Carter and LB Johnson, Queen Mum, Queen Liz II, Princess Margaret, Charles, Tony Blair, Prince Philip, and Zecharia Sitchin." She acknowledges that Starfire rituals go on as well. "In the underground vaults of his castle in the Alsace Region of France, green glowing fluorescent rocks turn stored menstrual blood black to be used at that special ritual. All the British House apparently have jewel-encrusted goblets to drink the blood from the symbolic female grail and a symbolic dagger to give it a bit of a stir. Some Spencers were at these rituals, but Diana would not attend... the smell of Diana's periods would have caused Charles to shapeshift - especially whilst sleeping because the reptiles cannot retain their human form without concentration." This may shed new light on Prince Charles' reported desire to become a tampon.

Aware of these charges, Laurence Gardner and Nicholas de Vere have tried to clear the record. They've acknowledged that vampirism does take place at their rituals, but maintain that they only drink the blood of their own family members, who participate willingly. "You cannot take the essences by force, they are only given in love", writes de Vere, otherwise, "their systems will react by producing chemicals during one's assault upon them that will completely knock out the chemicals traditionally required." He claims that vampirism was originally the purview of a few noble families who practiced it in order to maintain their powers. "The most famous stories", writes de Vere, "those of Dracula, Bathory and de Rais, support this conclusion." He and Gardner enthusiastically embrace Dracula as one of their own. "This Sacred Prince, a Hemetic scholar and initiate, a student of magic, Magus, Witch Lord and Dragon Prince, counterbalanced the bloodlust of his forebears with a refined knowledge and advanced practice of Grail procedure." This is because he was a member of Sigismund's Dragon Court in Hungary, and therefore of the Grail blood, and he also attended a hermetic academy called the Austrian School of Solomon. "The orthodox establishment's fear of Dracula," writes, Gardner, "was not his treatment of enemies but his in-depth knowledge of alchemy, kingship and the ancient Star

Fire customs." As for the claim that they use these rituals to conjure up dragon ancestors from another dimension, de Vere calmly admits that this is the case, and that the participants have their bodies taken over by these spirits, who "rise from the dead to take possession of the witch's soul!" He further explains that, "Any spirit, including the archangels, conjured by the witch or magician was actually the ancestor of the witch. ...It was carried in the witch's blood which, the purer it was through the unbroken descent from the Dragons, the stronger would be the return from the ancestors within. In other words, they brought together and spoke or gesticulated a series of mnemonics that would trigger off precontrived, imprinted states of consciousness that acted as doorways into deeper seats of consciousness." The charge of Satanism is not entirely refuted either, but de Vere proffers that they are not worshipping Satan so much as honoring one of their forefathers, who they stick right in the family tree along with Jesus, David and the rest. "The Sabbatical Goat of the Black Mass was Chem Zoroaster,", he writes, "one of the early ancestors of the ancient Dragon Families," and, "Satan was also called by the witches 'Christ, son Dei.' ...Jesus' heredity and the descent of he druidic dynasties...was devilish, because the descent of both bloodlines was from the Sumerian Enki who was the Akkadian Samael: the Roman Lucifer and thus the Catholic Satan." But the Dragon Court members make no apology for this, because, "To any intelligent person, to any true seer, concepts like white or black magic or good and evil are irrational, childish nonsense; both in terms of logic and actual fact."

Every Elf For Himself

"This is our Law, and the Law of the Strong."

-- Crowley, ibid.

To the charges of "conspiring to take over the world", the Dragons deny that they give two licks what the rest of humanity does with itself. Their primary concern is "the restoration of their own Tribes, their own Nation and their own Homelands.... the foundation of their own distinct society...re-introducing their old social structures and values." This results in "The Grail Code", a system of Egalitarian, Chivalric ethics that govern how dragons treat other members of their race. However, "it is not the code that efficiently orders the behaviour of the Dragon Families in their dealings with those not of the Grail Blood." They acknowledge and defend their own elitist attitudes towards mankind, whom they regard as "thoroughly stupid and dim-witted, with a clear indication that this condition is genetically inherited." Whereas in contrast, "The Elves were naturally transcendent of spirit and their queens and kings were insulated from the common round of nuisances and petty concerns by minds which were bred for deeper matters." Despite their hated of humanity, they will kindly agree to be the guardians of our governments again (if they aren't secretly doing so already), should the population choose to accept them, and offer them the thrones of the Earth, which de Vere and friends indicate are rightfully theirs anyway. They are just waiting for mankind to realize it again.

Whether we choose to or not, we will have to deal with the fact that these "Elves" seem to be in possession of a material that bestows long life as well as fantastic physical, mental, and spiritual powers, giving them a distinct advantage which they are clearly attempting to lord over us, while they allow our populations to wallow in disease, death, and spiritual degradation. As an excuse, de Vere and Gardner claim that the Starfire and White Gold are only effective for those already of the Dragon Blood anyway, because the rest of the people "won't have the right blood serum or the right connections in their cerebral lobes." De Vere denies the claims of most people who believe themselves to be of this bloodline. "Some people argue that because of the out-breeding of the old families, there must be millions of people 'of the fairy blood' living today: but such a statement flies in the face of accepted fact of history. The genuine old royal families rarely outbred at all, whilst the later, fake parvenu, tinker nobility whom people now confuse with them often did." So that leaves little hope for you and me of ever obtaining the fruits of this magnificent "Philosopher's Stone", which "gives youth to the old" and is described as " The summation of the heart's desire." And if such a substance were available to the public, how much would it cost? Would it be obtainable by everyone, or only the rich and privileged? What if it could be administered for free in the water supply, or was available in tablet form at your local pharmacy, covered by your health insurance policy? What would happen to our already exploding population? As a species, mankind will have to decide how to deal with the information - provided that the information is aired in public someday, and provided our "thoroughly stupid and dim-witted" populace can figure out what to do with it. Will we take advantage of what could be our greatest opportunity to advance as a species, or will we allow it to be used against us by a caste of Aryan overlords who despise us (and who are literally the spawn of Satan!) Then again, will we perhaps wish to accept their rule, and the benefits of being led by an advanced race whose powers and insight are greater than our own.? After all, there are those who believe that civilization is created by and can only be maintained by an established elite. Would we want to meddle with that, and allow positions of power to be overrun by inferior men? Perhaps it is worth considering whether an elite can truly be created by enhancing human faculties, or whether such powers are purely in the blood.

Michael Aquino's Response to Tracy Twyman's Request For an Interview

Here's Michael Aquino's response to Tracy Twyman's request for an interview about his purported involvement in Project Monarch.

8/23/01

"There is not really anything to "interview". Throughout my entire career as an Army officer (1968-94), I never encountered any evidence of anything named or resembling "Project Monarch", never participated in anything involving children [or adult] "sex slaves", never abused any children under any circumstances whatever, and never had any contact with any of the cranks who've thrown my name around with "Monarch". That's it, period.

To repeat the above with specific regard to any particular crackpot would simply serve to give his/her lies a dignity that they do not deserve, and I am not interested in doing that.

My impression of Hustler, though I haven't read it for many years now, is that, when it first came out, it contained (once one got past the graphic gynecology!) more than a few very brave, very blunt expose's of urban myths, political road muffins, and taboos that the "more respectable" media were too dainty to touch.

In particular I recall Hustler taking on the tobacco industry long before governments had the guts to do so. If its founder truly resembles his portrayal in The People vs. Larry Flynt, then more power to him!

In that tradition you can indeed put your foot down on the kind of creeps who use falsified allegations of "child abuse" to project their own disgusting sexual fantasies onto innocent third parties - and children - for nothing more than

cheap tabloid "glamour" and fraudulent financial scams.
That is the reality."

FACSIMILE: MK ULTRA Briefing Book

MKULTRA Briefing Book

Containing brief summaries
of each of the 149 MKULTRA subprojects

1 January 1976*

399 pages
(including cover sheet)

* Note: Document is undated. This is an <u>estimated</u> publication date.

RELEASED *January 1999*

OGC
Copy

Too little knowledge
on these 5 sub-projects:

80, 93, 141, 144,
145,

80 = $25 K
93 = $15 K
141 = $40 K
144 = $26 K
145 = $15.5 K

$121,500   Total

1

SECRET

SUB-PROJECT NO. 1

PRINCIPAL RESEARCHER AND LOCATION:
Princeton University

OBJECTIVE AND DETAILS OF WORK: To isolate and characterize the alkaloids of impomea sidaplia choisy (rivea corymbosa); to identify and characterize the agents affecting the central nervous system of human beings. ████████was to perform a literature search, chemically examine the seeds and their extracts for alkaloidal materials, and to determine specific methods for the isolation and purification of those alkaloids.

APPROXIMATE TIME SPAN: 1953-1954

SIGNIFICANT ASPECTS: None noted

FUNDING:

    COVER MECHANISM: Notional

    APPROXIMATE TOTAL: $1,300 in Sterile Cashier Check

RESEARCH PARTICIPANT: ██████████ - Witting

OTHERS: ████████had a ████Fellowship at Princeton during the time frame of this project. There is no indication in the file that ██████████was associated with or aware of Agency participation.

NAMES OF CIA MONITORS: Robert V. Lashbrook
████████████

APPROVERS: Sidney Gottlieb

        Willis A. Gibbons

        Luis deFlorez

SECRET

E2 IMPDET

2

Proj. 2

3

SECRET

SUB-PROJECT NO. 2 (See also Nos. 124 and 140)

PRINCIPAL RESEARCHER AND LOCATION: ██████████
██████████

OBJECTIVE AND DETAILS OF WORK: To do miscellaneous research and testing services in behavioral modification. Only two specific project proposals are contained in the file: The first is a proposal to study the possible synergistic action of drugs which may be appropriate for use in abolishing consciousness through animal experimentation, and, the second is a proposal for a survey of methods to enable the administration of drugs to patients without their knowledge. There is no record of project activity or results. Served as a contact and cut-out for projects in this field, primarily in the ██████████ Also monitored selected projects located in the ██████████ area and served as a general consultant and adviser. In addition, ██ ██████ acted as medical adviser and consultant to Mr. Morgan Hall.

APPROXIMATE TIME SPAN: 1953-1958

SIGNIFICANT ASPECTS: Animal testing is indicated in project proposals as a precondition to human testing. Human testing implied but money only requested for animal testing. File does not indicate whether human testing occurred or whether it was to be on volunteers or non-volunteers. As Morgan Hall believed

SECRET   E2 IMPDET
                 BY ██████

4

SECRET

SIGNIFICANT ASPECTS: (Continued)

to have been doing testing on unwitting subjects, it is likely

that ███████████ was on call for problems encountered by

Hall.

FUNDING:

    COVER MECHANISM: None

    APPROXIMATE TOTAL: $20,000 paid by check, both Treasury

    and Cashiers.

RESEARCH PARTICIPANT: ██████████████████, cleared TOP

SECRET, and on a contract basis - Witting.

OTHER SPONSORS: None indicated

NAMES OF CIA MONITORS: █████████████

                             Robert V. Lashbrook

APPROVERS: Sidney Gottlieb

              Willis A. Gibbons

              C. V. S. Roosevelt

2

SECRET

5

DRAFT/
11 August 1955

MEMORANDUM FOR: THE RECORD

SUBJECT : Project MKULTRA, Subproject 2A 2

1. Subproject 2⅔ is being initiated to provide a secure and efficient means of exploiting ███████ with regard to the MKULTRA program.

2. ████████ is a practicing psychiatrist in ███████, and a faculty member of Stanford Medical School. He has been of value in the general MKULTRA project, serving as an advisor and consultant, contacting individuals in the ██████ area, and carrying out his own research program.

3. Subproject 2⅔ would include the following:

(a) Miscellaneous research and testing services in the general field of MKULTRA.

(b) Services as a contact and cutout for projects in the MKULTRA field, primarily those located in the ██████ area.

(c) Monitoring of selected projects in the MKULTRA field, when located in the ██████ ██████ area.

(d) Services as a general consultant and advisor in the MKULTRA field.

(e) He would act as medical advisor and consultant to Mr. Morgan Hall and his ██████ establishment.

4. ████████ will be reimbursed for his services and expenses upon receipt of an invoice at irregular intervals. When travel expenses are incurred through use of a common carrier, they will be documented and reimbursed in the usual manner; that is, consistant with standard Government allowances.

6

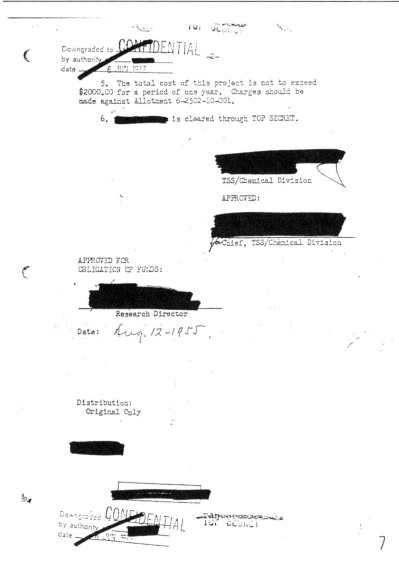

-2-

5. The total cost of this project is not to exceed $2000.00 for a period of one year. Charges should be made against Allotment 6-2502-10-001.

6. ███████ is cleared through TOP SECRET.

TSS/Chemical Division

APPROVED:

Chief, TSS/Chemical Division

APPROVED FOR
OBLIGATION OF FUNDS:

Research Director

Date: Aug. 12-1955

Distribution:
Original Only

7

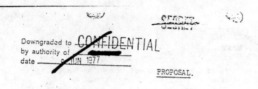

PROPOSAL.

Objective: To study the possible synergistic action of drugs which may be appropriate for use in abolishing consciousness.

Situation: There is reason to believe that two or more drugs, used in combination, are more effective than single drugs. The combined effect of some drugs, such as combinations of barbiturates, are known. With other combinations, the degree of synergism is not known. If considerable synergism is found to exist, two possibilities must be considered: (1) that a particularly useful combination may be found, and (2) that a particular combination may be hazardous because of its effect on respiration or some other vital function. To minimize hazards, animal experiments should precede human experiments.

Proposal: Allocation of $1000 for animal experiments, to be drawn on as needed. That experiments be conducted informally at Stanford without a specific grant, and with appropriate cover.

E. 2 IMPDET CL B

8

<u>PROPOSAL</u>

<u>Objective</u>: To study methods for the administration of drugs without the knowledge of the patient. Preparation of a manual.

<u>Method</u>: A survey of methods which have been used by criminals for surreptitious administration of drugs. Analysis of the psychodynamics of situations of this nature.

<u>Proposal</u>: That $1000 be allocated for this purpose, funds to be requested as needed.

9

Proj. 3.

10

SECRET

SUB-PROJECT NO. 3   (See also Nos. 16, 42, and 149)

PRINCIPAL RESEARCHER AND LOCATIONS: New York City and San
Francisco

OBJECTIVE AND DETAILS OF WORK: Realistic field testing

of R&D items of interest to TSS/CD.

APPROXIMATE TIME SPAN: 1953-1956

SIGNIFICANT ASPECTS: This is the project that started the

unwitting testing in New York.

FUNDING: $8,875 approved May 1953. Total: $8,875 in Cashier's

Checks.

RESEARCH PARTICIPANT: George White, aka Morgan Hall (alias)

"a seaman."

OTHER SPONSORS: None indicated.

NAMES OF CIA MONITORS: Sidney Gottlieb

Robert V. Lashbrook

APPROVERS: ██████████

Willia A. Gibbons

C.V.S. Roosevelt

E2 IMPDET

DE BY

11

SECRET

Proj. 4

12

SECRET

SUB-PROJECTS NUMBERS 4, 15, AND 19

PRINCIPAL RESEARCHER AND LOCATION: ▓▓▓▓▓▓▓

OBJECTIVE AND DETAILS OF WORK: All three of these projects are to fund the contractor, a magician, to write a manual on the various aspects of the magicians' art which could be useful in covert operations. One aspect of this project was to develop skills which could be used by the working field case officer to surreptitiously place a pill or other item in an item to be consumed by a target personality -- for example, a drinker.

A contractor was employed under Sub-Project No. 34 to prepare a paper on magicians techniques for the covert communication of information.

APPROXIMATE TIME SPAN: 1953-1954

SIGNIFICANT ASPECTS: One of the skills to be developed was the covert administration of drugs.

FUNDING:

COVER MECHANISM: None

APPROXIMATE TOTAL: $5,500, paid by sterile checks

RESEARCH PARTICIPANT: John Mulholland. Nowhere in the file does it specify that he is cleared and witting -- however, the deduction that he was completely witting is inescapable.

OTHER SPONSORS: None indicated

 SECRET

 E2 IMPDT
BY ▓▓▓▓

13

SECRET

NAMES OF CIA MONITORS: Sidney Gottlieb

Robert V. Lashbrook

APPROVERS: Sidney Gottlieb

Willis A. Gibbons

C. V. S. Roosevelt

James H. Drum

Luis deFlorez

2

SECRET

14

Proj. 5

15

SECRET

SUB-PROJECT NO. 5

PRINCIPAL RESEARCHER AND LOCATION: ██████████
        University of Minnesota,
        Later the University of Denver

OBJECTIVE AND DETAILS OF WORK: Work apparently began with a

demonstration in a ██████████████ hotel designed to

"demonstrate potentialities of hypnosis as a tool of the

clandestine services". Following the successful demonstration

this eventually evolved into Sub-Project No. 5. Research in

hypnosis was to determine if: hypnosis could be used as a memory

enhancer, a learning aid, a polygraph deceiver, etc. Also,

research into susceptibility of certain personality types to

hypnosis.

APPROXIMATE TIME SPAN: 1953-1956

SIGNIFICANT ASPECTS: None

FUNDING:

    COVER MECHANISM: Geschickter Fund

    APPROXIMATE TOTAL: $12,000 per year

RESEARCH PARTICIPANT: None

OTHER SPONSORS: None

NAMES OF CIA MONITORS: ██████████

APPROVERS: Sidney Gottlieb

 SECRET   E2 IMPDET
                                      CL BY ██████

16

Proj. 6

17

SUB-PROJECT NO. 6

PRINCIPAL RESEARCHERS AND LOCATIONS: Eli Lilly Company,
Indianapolis, Indiana

OBJECTIVES AND DETAILS OF WORK:

1. To develop reliable source of LSD within the United States.

2. To assist in the search for additional natural hypnotic products.

APPROXIMATE TIME SPAN: 1953-1955

SIGNIFICANT ASPECTS: Probably none. Object was to develop a domestic source for LSD. No testing was done.

FUNDING:

COVER MECHANISM: None

APPROXIMATE TOTAL: $5,000 was approved but not expended as Eli Lilly Company did not charge for this work.

RESEARCH PARTICIPANT: ████████████ (Eli Lilly Company) - witting.

OTHER SPONSOR: None

NAMES OF CIA MONITORS: Sidney Gottlieb

Robert V. Lashbrook

APPROVERS: Willis A. Gibbons

C.V.S. Roosevelt

Luis de Florez

18

Proj. 7

19

SUB-PROJECTS NUMBERS 7, 27 and 40

PRINCIPAL RESEARCHER AND LOCATIONS: Dr. Harold A. Abramson, who sponsored work at two locations:

OBJECTIVES AND DETAILS OF WORK: This work started prior to MKULTRA with RO-37 in 1952 and was carried forward with Sub-Projects 7, 1953-1954; 27, 1954-1955, and 40, 1956. These projects seem to be the nucleus of the LSD program and the three were done at both locations. Dr. Abramson, as well as doing work himself, subcontracted research to other specialists. The first years' work seemed aimed at characterizing the various effects of LSD with the aim of ultimately producing a manual for field use. During Sub-Project No. 7, money was provided to sub-contract "work in the fields of brain enzyme and nerve metabolism." As an indication of the scope: "Another psychiatrist will independently analyze the verbatim recordings in over 100 experiments in which LSD-25 has already been given." Sub-Projects No. 27 continued the earlier emphasis to understand the total effects of LSD by studying "tissue metabolism" and LSD influence on embryological development. In addition, work was undertaken to look for LSD antidotes and blocking agents. Sub-Project No. 40 continued the previous work and added aerosol delivery studies. Basic documents on each of the three projects are attached.

E2 IMPDET

L BY

APPROXIMATE TIME SPAN: 1952-1956

SIGNIFICANT ASPECTS: The work appears to be the necessary
basic research on a drug whose impact on society was just beginning.
The studies included the use of LSD in therapy. As far as is
known, subjects in this experimentation were witting. Funds are
included for the payment of subjects. Sub-Project No. 7's
proposal contains the following quotation:

> "One of the difficulties of determining explicitly
> the effect of the drug itself is that the subject
> and the observer are both conscious of the fact that
> an experiment is being performed. It is hoped that,
> in the next year, subjects on the ███████████████
> who are essentially normal from a psychiatric point
> of view, will be given unwitting doses of the drug
> for psychotherapeutic purposes. In this way more
> valuable experiments will probably be carried out
> in spite of hospital conditions."

It is not known whether unwitting, in this case, meant fully
unwitting or unwitting as to timing. It is also unknown
whether unwitting doses were actually given.

FUNDING:

    COVER MECHANISM: Geschickter Foundation for Medical
                     Research

    APPROXIMATE TOTAL: $205,000

- 2 -

SECRET

RESEARCH PARTICIPANTS: Dr. Harold A. Abramson, Witting.

████████████████ Dr. Abramson,
Witting.

██████████, Unknown if Witting.

██████████ Unknown if Witting.

██████████ Unknown if Witting.

█████████Unknown if Witting.

██████████, Unknown if Witting.

Other names, believed to be clerical,
were included.

Money went to the institutions from whom the researchers drew
salaries. As the funding was contributed through a cut-out, it
is unlikely that the institutions' administrators as a group
knew that the CIA was its ultimate source.

OTHER SPONSORS: ███████████, Public Health Service,
and ██████████, Unknown if Witting.

NAMES OF CIA MONITORS: Sidney Gottlieb

███████████

APPROVERS: Luis deFlorez

Willis A. Gibbons

C.V.S. Roosevelt

- 3 -

SECRET

22

HAROLD A. ABRAMSON, M.D.

(40)

June 12, 1956

Dear ▮▮▮

     May I thank you for the interest shown by your Company in the project at ▮▮▮▮▮▮ I should like to enlist your aid, if I may, for continuation of the project along the following lines.

     1. Aerosol Studies. The therapy of individuals by means of aerosols is of great significance in medicine. A hitherto unexplored area of aerosols is the delivery of nebulizers using nonaqueous solvents. It is proposed that studies be made of organic materials in non-aqueous solvents and their mixtures with water to determine nebulizer delivery over prolonged periods of therapy. (60 per cent of budget).

     2. As you know, the blocking of LSD reactions has been claimed by many pharmaceutical houses, although none of these claims have really been substantiated. It is proposed that recent investigations by me on tissue extracts be further explored with a view toward discovering what it is in these extracts that blocks the LSD reaction, keeping in mind possible application of these compounds to experimental and clinical psychoses in man. It is understood that this part of the project will be discontinued December 31, 1956. (20 per cent of budget).

c-487
23

- 2 -

        3. Continuation of studies on non-psychotic humans with a view toward maintaining a test group, as well as to provide experimental work in a frame of reference different from that frame of reference incorporated by items 1. and 2. of the foregoing. However, it shall be the primary purpose of the nonpsychotic test group to test the results obtained by items 1. and 2. (20 per cent of budget).

        It is anticipated that the foregoing budget may be amplified by supplementary funds to be received from foundations.

        The following is the proposed budget. Owing to the uncertainty of plans for the fiscal year 1956-1957, I should like, if possible, to have the privilege of utilizing the proposed budget to September 30, 1957 rather than to June 30, 1957.

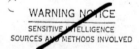

WARNING NOTICE
SENSITIVE INTELLIGENCE
SOURCES AND METHODS INVOLVED

24

- 3 -

<u>Proposed Budget</u>

Salaries			29,950
A. Professional		15,000	
1. Principal Investigator	8,500		
2. Biophysicist or			
Physical Chemist	6,500		
B. Technical		7,950	
1. Research Assistant	4,750		
2. Biologist	3,200		
C. Secretarial-Editorial		7,000	
Expendable Supplies			1,550
Fish, chemicals, glassware,			
photography, telephone,			
stationery			
Experiments on Man			4,000
Payment of subjects, food,			
professional assistance			
Travel			1,000
Overhead			3,500
			40,000

      With many thanks and hoping for your
continued support, I am,

                Yours sincerely,

                Harold A. Abramson, M. D.

HAA:█

25

Security Information

Downgraded to CONFIDENTIAL
by authority of
date ___ JUN 1977

DRAFT
9 June 1953

#7

MEMORANDUM FOR THE RECORD

SUBJECT: Project MKULTRA, Subproject 7

1. The scope of subproject 7 is intended to include the work
to be done with LSD and related materials by Dr. Harold A. Abramson
at his two facilities for the period ending July 4, 1954. The project
will continue to be handled through the Geschickter Foundation for
cut-out and cover purposes. The proposal from Dr. Abramson to the
Geschickter Foundation is attached to this memorandum.

2. Emphasis will be placed in this coming year on translating the
basic data obtained to date into operationally pertinent material along
the following lines:

   a. Disturbance of Memory
   b. Discrediting by Aberrant Behavior
   c. Alteration of Sex Patterns
   d. Eliciting of Information
   e. Suggestibility
   f. Creation of Dependence

It is planned to have the second year's work culminate in a
compendium of information on this subject that will resemble an
operational field manual as much as possible. All other CD/TSS project
data that has a bearing on this subject will be used in the preparation
of the manual.

3. The sum of money listed under Dr. Abramson's budget includes
work in the fields of brain enzyme work and nerve metabolism to be
subcontracted to other organizations.

4. The funds include $45,650 for the project at ███████
█████, $39,500 for Dr. Abramson's own project, and a 2% service
charge for the Geschickter Foundation amounting to $1703.00.
Therefore, the total cost of this investigation will not exceed
$86,853.00 for the period from July 5, 1953 to July 4, 1954.

SIDNEY GOTTLIEB
Chief
Chemical Division, TSS

PROGRAM

Downgraded to CONFIDENTIAL
authority of
date 6 JUN 1977

Security Information

26

Downgraded to ████████ Security Information
by authority of
date ___6___ 1977

PROGRAM APPROVED
AND RECOMMENDED:

████████

Research Chairman

Date: _____

Attachment:
Proposal

Original Only.

APPROVED FOR OBLIGATION
OF FUNDS:

████████

Research Director

Date: *June 10-1953*

-2-

Downgraded ████ CONFIDENTIAL
by author ████ 1977   TOP SECRET
date ████   Security Information   E.... REPORT CL BY ████

27

HAROLD A. ABRAMSON, M. D.

~~SECRET~~
SECURITY INFORMATION

Downgraded ~~CONFIDENTIAL~~
by auth..
dat.. ~~6 JUN 1977~~

June 8, 1953

Charles F. Geschickter, M. D.
Geschickter Fund for Medical Research, Inc.
1834 Connecticut Avenue, N. W.
Washington 9, D. C.

Dear Dr. Geschickter:

    May I acknowledge with thanks the support of your
Foundation for the previous year's research on LSD25. I should
like to take this opportunity to apply for support for the fiscal
year July 5, 1953 to July 4, 1954 to continue the research project
on the effect of LSD25 on normal adults. The program for the
following year is planned as follows:

    Content analysis of the present data will be attempted
by two psychiatrists. One of these psychiatrists will be the
psychiatrist assigned to the project itself. This psychiatrist
has observed the phenomena. Another psychiatrist will independently
analyze the verbatim recordings in over 100 experiments in which
LSD25 has already been given. A comparison of the two surveys will
be made to evaluate not only the effects of the drug but the technique
of the experimental procedures. The analysis of the data will first
concern itself with the raw material and the significance of individual and group responses based on the raw material as presented by

CONFIDENTIAL

Downgraded to
by authority of

~~SECRET~~

28

FACSIMILE: Behavioral Drugs and Tests

4/60

1 7 ... 1975

Behavioral Drugs, and Testing

1. CIA has had a recurring interest in behavioral drugs. The subject is of general interest because of the operational applications that could be made against Agency employees by hostile forces, for which there would be a defensive requirement, as well as for possible use against foreigners to influence their behavior. The earliest record of this interest dates to the post-WWII period when there were indications of Soviet interest in the use of drugs for such purposes, the most famous example being the bizarre confessions of Cardinal Mindszenty in February 1949.

2. In the past CIA's interest in behavioral drugs was expressed in at least three programs, which have been identified. These programs apparently proceeded on largely independent courses, subject to some informal coordination by a group referred to as the ARTICHOKE Committee, which started in April 1952. This mechanism provided the means for exchanging information and for deciding which components would assume responsibility for certain study and research. Representation on the ARTICHOKE Committee was from the Offices of Scientific Intelligence (OSI) and Medical Services (OMS) and the predecessor organizations of the Offices of Security (OS) and Technical Services (OTS). The ARTICHOKE Committee initially was concerned with drugs that would assist in interrogation, but the concept expanded to include drugs that would serve as a defense against hostile application to Agency employees as well as drugs that would afford some control when administered to an individual. Remaining records, which are not complete, refer to sodium pentothal and sodium amytal, as well as LSD.

BLUEBIRD/ARTICHOKE

3. In 1949 the Office of Scientific Intelligence (OSI) undertook the analysis of foreign work on certain unconventional warfare techniques, including behavioral drugs, with an initial objective of developing a capability to resist or offset the effect of behavioral drugs. Preliminary phases included the review of drug-related work at institutions such as

There also was extensive review of foreign literature, particularly work

DATE, SUBJECT, PARAGRAPH 8 AND IDENS 6-12 ARE DECLASSIFIED BY AUTHORITY OF THE DCI ON 24 JULY 1975. THE BALANCE OF THIS DOCUMENT RETAINS ITS SECRET CLASSIFICATION AND SENSITIVE DESIGNATION.

75-93

In the Soviet Bloc. This program shortly became Project BLUEBIRD with the objectives of (a) discovering means of conditioning personnel to prevent unauthorized extraction of information from them by known means, (b) investigating the possibility of obtaining control of an individual by application of special interrogation techniques, (c) memory enhancement, and (d) establishing defensive means for preventing hostile control of Agency personnel.

4. In August 1951 Project BLUEBIRD was renamed Project ARTICHOKE which, in 1952, was transferred from OSI to the predecessor organization of the Office of Security. OSI did retain a responsibility for evaluation of foreign intelligence aspects of the matter and in 1953 made a proposal that experiments be made in testing LSD with Agency volunteers; OSI records indicate that no such experiments were made. OSI's involvement in this project was terminated in 1956. Meanwhile, the emphasis given ARTICHOKE in the predecessor organization to the Office of Security became that of use of materials such as sodium pentothal in connection with interrogation techniques and with the polygraph.

5. There are references to ARTICHOKE Teams travelling to Europe and East Asia during the 1950s, for the apparent purpose of interrogation of foreign agents, but the results of such operations are not revealed by existing records.

MKDELTA/MKULTRA/MKSEARCH

6. On 29 October 1952 a formal policy was established by the Deputy Director of Plans (as then styled, now Deputy Director for Operations) for the use of biochemicals in clandestine operations (MKDELTA). This was in anticipation of the development of behavioral drugs, but was never implemented operationally. MKDELTA research was brought under a special funding procedure established on 3 April 1953 (MKULTRA). The program considered various possible means for controlling human behavior of which drugs were only one aspect, others being radiation, electroshock, psychology, psychiatry, sociology, anthropology, harrassment substances, and paramilitary devices and materials. There were contacts with individuals at such institutions as the ▓▓▓▓▓▓▓▓▓▓▓▓▓▓▓▓▓▓▓ and the ▓▓▓▓▓▓▓▓▓▓▓▓ as well as with various pharmaceutical houses, hospitals and federal institutions, the names of which are no longer available.

- 2 -

75-44

Among the materials studied were psylocbin from Mexican mushrooms, a fungus occurring in certain crops, and LSD. Following laboratory testing a second phase was begun which involved testing on voluntary participants. The final phase involved application on unwitting subjects, in normal social situations, commencing in 1955 under an informal arrangement with individuals in the Bureau of Narcotics. Originally conducted on the West Coast, a similar arrangement was instituted in 1961 on the East Coast. Such tests were conducted from time to time until 1963 when the Inspector General discovered the activity and questioned the program. At that time it was reported that in a number of instances test subjects became ill for hours or days following the application, and there was one reported instance of hospitalization, the details of which are no longer available. Project records do not now exist, but it is reported that the project was decreased significantly each budget year until it was completely terminated in the late 1960's.

7. Follwing the Inspector General's challenge of the program, there was a review of its nature and it was resubmitted for approval under the name of Project MKSEARCH. The written proposal did not specify whether testing was to be limited to volunteers. Records indicate that the DCI did not approve unwitting testing; it is understood that there was no renewal of this aspect of the activity. Funding for MKSEARCH commenced in FY-1966, running through 1972. There were various research activities carried on under it, but the only aspect related to behavioral drugs deal with an inquiry in improvement by drugs of learning ability and memory retention; under this there is a record of testing at Iden 1 State Prison in Iden 5 , on volunteers.

Drug-related Death of an Investigator

8. The predecessor organization of the Office of Technical Service was the focal point for the operational investigation of behavioral drugs, although none of the office's records on this activity are in existence, having been destroyed in January 1973. As noted above it participated in the meetings of the so-called ARTICHOKE Committee. That office maintained liaison with personnel at Iden 6 , with whom meetings were held once or twice a year to discuss questions involving behavioral drugs. At one such meeting at Iden 7 in Maryland, Iden 8 1953, with seven representatives from Iden 6 : and three from CIA, eight of those present were administered LSD which had been introduced into a bottle of Cointreau. Although records of an inquiry by the Inspector General into the incident indicate that those present

- 3 -

460

discussed testing on unwitting persons, and agreed in principle
that such a program should be explored, none of them were advised
until some 20 minutes after they drank the Cointreau that it had
been treated with LSD. Of the two who did not take it, one did
not drink alcoholic beverages at all and the other refrained because of a heart condition. One of the members of the group, a
civilian employee of the Department of Army named Iden 9, had
serious after-effects. He was sent at CIA expense, with an
escort from CIA to New York where he received treatment
from a psychiatrist, commencing Iden 10. While in New York for
this treatment he threw himself through a closed window in his room
on the tenth floor of the Iden 11, falling to his death. CIA, in a
document of Iden 12, signed by its General Counsel, certified Iden 9
death resulted from "circumstances arising out of an experiment
undertaken in the course of his official duties for the United States
Government." This was the official position of the Agency, established
for the purpose of assuring that the survivors of Iden 9 received com-
pensation from the BEC. Iden 9 had experienced some instability and
delusions prior to the incident, and it was judged that the drug served
to trigger the act leading to his death. Reprimands were issued by
the DCI to two CIA employees held responsible for the incident.

OFTEN/CHICKWIT

9. In 1967 the Office of Research and Development (ORD) and
the Edgewood Arsenal Research Laboratories undertook a program for
doing research on the identification and characterization of drugs that
could influence human behavior. Edgewood had the facilities for the
full range of laboratory and clinical testing. A phased program was
envisioned that would consist of acquisition of drugs and chemical
compounds believed to have effects on the behavior of humans, and
testing and evaluating these materials through laboratory procedures
and toxicological studies. Compounds believed promising as a result
of tests on animals were then to be evaluated clinically with human
subjects at Edgewood. Substances of potential use would then be
analyzed structurally as a basis for identifying and synthesizing
possible new derivatives of greater utility.

- 4 -

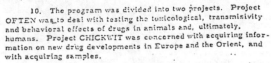

460

10. The program was divided into two projects. Project OFTEN was to deal with testing the toxicological, transmissivity and behavioral effects of drugs in animals and, ultimately, humans. Project CHICKWIT was concerned with acquiring information on new drug developments in Europe and the Orient, and with acquiring samples.

11. Samples of drugs and chemicals were obtained from drug and pharmaceutical companies, government agencies such as Edgewood, NIH, FDA and the Veterans Administration, as well as from research laboratories and individual researchers. Most of the materials came from the drug industry, consisting largely of substances that had been rejected because of undesired side effects from the point of view of medicinal use.

12. A panel was established to review the program, with membership from ████, and the predecessor organization of the ████████████████ Meetings were held periodically, and briefings were given senior officials from time to time. The principal contractor under OFTEN was Iden 2, commencing FY-1966. The association with Edgewood started with a transfer of funds to Edgewood in FY-1967, for work to be done by Iden 3 under CHICKWIT. Synthesis of new drugs and derivatives was contracted with Iden 4, starting FY-1971. Data from this program was merged ████████████████████████████ with test data and information from other sources. One substance identified as a potential incapacitant was in an area known to be the subject of research by the Soviet Union, being considered a potential threat to U. S. leaders because of the ease with which it could be administered.

13. CIA's program was terminated in January 1973, its final billing from Edgewood being received in April of that year. Edgewood did not progress to testing materials on human volunteer subjects under the work sponsored by CIA.

14. With CIA's termination of the program, the program data was withdrawn ████████████████████████ and limited records being sequestered and stores under special controls where they still are.

- 5 -

75-97

INFLUENCING HUMAN BEHAVIOR

460

ACTIVITY: Factors Influencing Human Behavior

PROGRAMS: To understand and identify factors which contribute or are believed to contribute to influencing human behavior. The studies fall into three categories: (a) personality factors; (b) techniques; and (c) methods to detect whether or not the techniques have been used. The categories are inter-active, that is, it is impossible to do studies in category (c) without also going through procedures (b) and selection procedure which fall in category (a).

Because the terms "influencing behavior" or "controlling behavior" can readily be misconstrued, it is important to define the terms and to understand the procedures that were pursued, how and by whom. By "influence and control" is meant increasing the probability of occurrence of an outcome at least for predictive purposes. Techniques that have been examined are ▬▬▬▬▬▬▬▬▬▬▬▬▬ In each instance, our projects effectively supplemented a research program that was already on-going in the principal investigator's facility, which was being funded by non-Agency sources and the results of which had already been published, at least, in part in the open pro-fessional literature. In short, the unofficial or at least not-formalized policy has been to identify acknowledged expertise through open professional literature and supplement already on-going research programs. None of the work has been classified, the association with the Agency commonly was classified. Com-pleted studies of the research have been published without acknow-ledgment of Agency sponsorship.

CONTRACTOR: Iden 1,
1965-1967

CONTRACTOR: Iden 1,
1974

75-98

INFLUENCING HUMAN BEHAVIOR (continued)

A great many of the Behavioral Science research projects are dependent upon human volunteer subjects. Current practice is to adhere strictly to the HEW guidelines concerning the use of human subjects and all current contracts carry language to that effect, as well as assurances that the anonymity of volunteer subjects will be maintained. Prior to the existence of the published HEW guidelines, the working policy followed by was to have the principal investigators adhere to the institutic professional, and ethics criteria that were ordinarily used. In short, research subjects being used on Agency-sponsored researc? were to be treated no differently than research subjects on projects sponsored by other U.S. Government or private groups.

2

75-99

FACSIMILE: Mind-Behavior Control

5 March 1973

MEMORANDUM FOR:

SUBJECT   : Mind/Behavior Control

1. The purpose of this memorandum is to succinctly outline the various techniques that fall under the rubric of "mind" or "behavior control" (paragraph 2) and to indicate which projects has supported, is currently supporting, or is considering for support that may be misconstrued as having the control of others as the primary goal (paragraph 3). The terms "mind control" or "behavior control" can be interpreted in context of controlling others or controlling self; the question of ethics is likely to arise if the former interpretation is used. Whatever interpretation is used, the techniques are not as efficacious or finely tuned as the popular media leads one to believe. Lastly, one should bear in mind that most of the techniques are still experimental in nature and have as a primary goal the understanding of brain-behavior relations which in turn may lead to "control" in the sense of therapeutic intervention or patient management.

2. The following techniques are generally considered under "control" technology:

a. Psychosurgery - direct intervention into the neurological pathways that mediate or control behavior. The procedure may be non-reversible (surgical extirpation) or reversible (electrical stimulation). This approach has received a great deal of publicity recently in context of surgery being performed to control aggressive behavior.

b. Psychopharmacology - behavioral control is achieved by altering the brain chemistry. Tranquilizers and energizers are the two most common classes. This technique is widely used in clinical medicine. The technique is for the most part safe and effective but does not really afford fine control. The notion of a "peace" pill, "truth" pill or "smart" pill is still in the wish stage.

SUBJECT: Mind/Behavior Control

c. Behavior modification - this term refers to alterations in behavior that are achieved by using conditioning techniques, usually variations on operant or performance conditioning. The behavior being altered or controlled can be either external (behavior) or internal (autonomic or central nervous system) responses. The conditioning or control of internal response (biofeedback), particularly those of the central nervous system, e.g., alpha waves, has received much publicity as mind control with fantastic claims for its utility. While there is no doubt that the physiological responses are indeed controllable (within limits), there is no good evidence that the desired behavioral concomitants are automatically changed, i.e., creativity increased. On the other hand, there is some evidence that control of autonomic nervous system functions may have some therapeutic utility, e.g., control of cardiac arrhythmias or hypertension, again within limits.

d. Education - the most innocuous, most effective and acceptable means of effecting behavioral control or change is education. The educative process which includes propaganda techniques, does not merely transmit information but a belief or value system as well. It is the latter which often provides the impetus to dramatic and difficult to understand behaviors, e.g., suicidal terrorist activities.

e. Special techniques:

(1) Hypnosis and self-hypnosis (autogensis) - this is a real but very poorly understood phenomena. Contrary to popular belief, hypnosis is effective only with very cooperative and suggestible subjects. Much is dependent upon the belief system of the subject, particularly in self-hypnosis. Except with rare subjects, the technique does not appear uniformly reliable. Of late, hypnosis and biofeedback are being tied together apparently on the simple premise that two is better than one. There is no good evidence for or against this linkage.

(2) ESP - interest in this area is on the upswing again, in large part due to current popularity in lay literature of "biofeedback" technology. The basic premise appears to be that all individuals (or most) have "ESP" as a latent capability

-2-

SUBJECT: Mind/Behavior Control

and that biofeedback programs will allow it to become manifest. This then becomes the route to "mind control" in the sense that the individual will have at his beck and call telepathic, clairvoyant, psychokinetic or other unusual capabilities. The claims are made by companies offering training programs, marketing biofeedback equipment or both. Thus far, no evidence (other than testimonials) has surfaced which substantiates these claims.

3. Past, present, or planned _____ projects by category as in paragraph 2, which may be misconstrued as a CIA program in mind or behavior control:

a. Psychosurgery - _____ has supported a basic research project on the Localization of Memory Processes. The experimental animal is the rhesus monkey; selected areas of the animals prefrontal lobes are surgically removed and the animal is tested to determine its ability to "remember" old tasks and/or to learn new ones. This class of research has been going on in academia for over 35 years and is deemed "respectable" in that setting. There are no renewal plans upon the expiration of the current contract with _____
_____ This research has been UNCLASSIFIED.

b. Psychopharmacology - the OFTEN program fell into this category. The objective of the MATERIALS ANALYSIS/OFTEN program was to develop the capability of detecting and nullifying the use of psychoactive drugs on U.S. personnel abroad. The central project in the program was the maintenance of a facility to determine the biological and behavioral activity of certain compounds in mice, rats, and monkeys. Per direction, all OFTEN projects have been cancelled and are in various phaseout stages. Association with the Agency has been classified; major contractor was the _____

c. Behavior modification:

(1) Operant conditioning, biofeedback - no work in this area has been supported in the past. Biofeedback will be examined in context of the _____ program. Association with the Agency will be classified; probable contractor is the _____

-3-

SUBJECT: Mind/Behavior Control

(2) ⌐‾‾‾‾‾⌐ Studies - this is an on-going
project whose goal is to determine whether the
potential can be used as an indicator that an individual may
have undergone some "conditioning" process impinging on his
value system. The ⌐‾‾‾‾‾⌐ is the contractor,
work and association are UNCLASSIFIED.

d. Education - no ⌐‾‾⌐ activities; some past work in support
of ⌐‾⌐ e.g., program assisted instruction studies.

e. Special techniques:

(1) Hypnosis - past involvement was to use expertise of
a contractor (who had been tasked to examine other things) to
stay abreast of developments in the field. Current plans call
for preliminary work on hypnosis in context of the⌐‾‾‾⌐
⌐‾‾‾⌐ program. Probable contractor is the⌐‾‾‾⌐
⌐‾‾‾⌐ association with the Agency will
be classified but the work will be UNCLASSIFIED.

(2) ESP - the basic position⌐‾‾⌐ has taken has been to
stay abreast of the developments through the use of a personal
services contract. Apart from the monitoring effort, ⌐did
support ⌐‾‾‾⌐ a project with ⌐‾‾‾⌐
⌐‾⌐ on coincident EEG's in twins. Results were negative.
Plans for future active research are uncertain but are likely
to be a cooperative endeavor with⌐‾‾‾⌐ (in context of
current program at⌐‾‾‾⌐

-4-

Project Summary

19 December 1966

4.   Sleep   and sleep learning. studies are continuing with no problems. Data is suggestive but not particularly exciting.

Illustrations

ALEX HOUSTON and ELMER

NASHVILLE'S BEST

Dr. Ewen Cameron

Dr. Sidney Gottlieb

Josef Rudolf Mengele

The Washington Times

THURSDAY, JUNE 29, 1989 •

WASHINGTON, D.C.

PHONE (202) 636-3000 **25 cents**
SUBSCRIBER SERVICE (202) 636-3333

SUNNY
HIGH 84, LOW 67, PAGE B6

Homosexual prostitution inquiry ensnares VIPs with Reagan, Bush

'Call boys' took midnight tour of White House

By Paul M. Rodriguez
and George Archibald
THE WASHINGTON TIMES

A homosexual prostitution ring is under investigation by federal and District authorities and includes among its clients key officials of the Reagan and Bush administrations, military officers, congressional aides and U.S. and foreign businessmen with close social ties to Washington's political elite, documents obtained by The Washington Times reveal.

One of the ring's high-profile clients was so well-connected, in fact, that he could arrange a middle-of-the-night tour of the White House for his friends on Sunday, July 3, of last year. Among the six persons on the extraordinary 1 a.m. tour were two male prostitutes.

Federal authorities, including the Secret Service, are investigating

criminal aspects of the ring and have told male prostitutes and their homosexual clients that a grand jury will deliberate over the evidence throughout the summer, The Times learned.

Reporters for this newspaper examined hundreds of credit-card vouchers, drawn on both corporate and personal cards and made payable to the escort service operated by the homosexual ring. Many of the vouchers were run through a sophisticated "sub-merchant" account of the Chambers Funeral Home by a son of the owner, without the company's knowledge.

Among the client names contained in the vouchers — and later verified by private investigators and interviews — are government officials, locally based U.S. military officers,

homosexuals, lawyers, bankers, congressional aides and other private citizens.

Editors of The Times said the newspaper would print only the

names of those found to be in sensitive government posts or positions of influence. "There is no intention of publishing names or facts about the operation merely for titillation,"

said Wesley Pruden, managing editor of The Times.

The office of U.S. Attorney Jay B. Stephens, former deputy White House counsel to President Reagan, is coordinating federal aspects of the inquiry but refused to discuss the investigation or grand jury action.

Several former White House colleagues of Mr. Stephens are listed among clients of the homosexual prostitution ring, according to the credit-card records, and these persons have confirmed that the charges were theirs.

Mr. Stephens' office, after first saying it would cooperate with The Times inquiry, withdrew the offer. He yesterday said also declined to say whether Mr. Stephens would recuse himself from the case because of possible conflict of interest.

At least one highly placed Bush administration official and a wealthy businessman who procured homosexual prostitutes from the escort service operated by the ring are cooperating with the investigation, sources said.

Among clients who are charged homosexual prostitute services on major credit cards over the past 18 months are Charles K. Dutcher, former associate director of presidential personnel in the Reagan administration, and Paul R. Balach, Labor Secretary Elizabeth Dole's political personnel liaison to the White House.

In the 1970s, Mr. Dutcher was a congressional aide to former Rep. Robert Bauman, Maryland Republican, who resigned from the House after he admitted having sexual liaisons with teen-age boys.

see PROBE, page A7

EX-GREEN BERET Lieut
Col. Michael Aquino is
a high priest of a sa-
tanic church

Gary Condit

Virginia McMartin

Lawrence E. King Jr

Paul Bishop

Jeff Gannon

John David Gosch

Paul Bonacci

Hunter S. Thompson